EUCHARIST IN THE LOCAL CHURCH

by Neil Darragh
in association with Jo Ayers

EUCHARIST IN THE LOCAL CHURCH:
Meeting the challenge of real participation

by Neil Darragh
in association with Jo Ayers

ATF Theology
Adelaide

2012

Text copyright © 2012 remains with Neil Darragh and Jo Ayers.

All rights reserved. Except for any fair dealing permitted under the Copyright Act, no part of this book may be reproduced by any means without prior permission. Inquiries should be made to the publisher.

ISBN: 9781921817854

Artwok and front cover artwork by Yvonne Ashby
Layout and design Anna Dimasi
Text Minion Pro Size 11

Published by:

An imprint of the ATF Ltd
PO Box 504
Hindmarsh, SA 5007
ABN 90 116 359 963
www.atfpress.com

Contents

	Introduction	vii
1.	Active Participation	1
2.	The Current Context	11
3.	The Christian Assembly and its Ministries	23
4.	The Rites of Gathering and Sending	35
5.	The Liturgy of the Word	45
6.	The Liturgy of Eucharist	59
7.	Liturgical Leadership	73
8.	Liturgical Music	85
9.	The Liturgical Calendar	99
10.	Related Liturgies	111
11.	Eucharist in the Local Church	123
	Index	133

Introduction

This book is about *active participation in Sunday Eucharist*. It is intended as an aid to liturgical planners, priests, and ministers in communities where active participation is highly valued. Our focus is on perspectives and principles that make a difference to how we do our liturgies and on the challenges that currently face liturgical planners.

The book occupies a middle ground between the purely practical and the largely theoretical. We do not intend it as a manual for new ministers on the one hand or a study in liturgical theology on the other[1]. It does not deal, for example, with the practicalities of how to read scripture in church. Nor, on the other hand, does it deal with the deeper Christian understanding of scripture as the word of God. But, to continue with the present example, it does attempt to deal with how the reading of scripture may change people's lives when they gather for Eucharist.

There are many collections of liturgical resources available elsewhere both in handbooks and on the internet. Many of these provide useful hints and stimulants for liturgical planners and ministers. This book is not intended as a handy toolkit of such resources. It does nevertheless give illustrations and examples of how the principles advocated here can work in practice. All the examples presented in this book are real in the sense that they have already been tried somewhere at some time by someone. In presenting our own examples we invite readers to respond with creative applications for their own situations.

---

1. Readers who do seek more understanding of liturgical theology may usefully consult Catherine Vincie, *Celebrating Divine Mystery: A Primer in Liturgical Theology* (Collegeville, Minnesota: Liturgical Press, 2009). For a substantial theological and pastoral explanation of Eucharist, traditionally based but also focused on contemporary (American) concerns, see Kevin W. Irwin, *Models of the Eucharist* (New York/Mahwah: Paulist Press, 2005).

An appreciation of cultural differences lies at the heart of liturgical creativity in local communities. It is this appreciation that distinguishes local community planners and ministers from those who have a larger scale international responsibility for texts and rubrics such as those in the Roman Missal. A key to success for local planners in their focus on community participation in Eucharist is the recognition that the impact of symbolic actions may differ from one community to another.

Symbolic actions may have a different meaning, and therefore a different impact, depending on the mixture of cultures and traditions that make up a local Christian community. Gestures of greeting or words of welcome, for example, often have different meanings in different cultures. The same gesture or the same set of words when used in different cultural settings can create very different atmospheres in community gatherings. Gestures and words that seem warm and respectful in one culture are cold and formal in another. And so it is to local liturgical planners who work out of sensitivity and respect for their own local traditions and cultures that this book is addressed.

Where does this book sit in the larger picture?

There are approaches to the planning and celebration of Eucharist that do not focus upon active participation. Two other, and opposite, approaches are those where the major concern is the central role of the priest in Eucharist and where the major concern is the popular nature of worship.

An approach to liturgy that is concerned principally with the role of the priest emphasizes the idea of the ordained minister as presider or mediator between God and the congregation. It maintains a clear distinction between the priest as principal actor in the liturgy and the congregation as recipients of the priest's mediation and service. It retains a clear boundary between the sanctuary and the nave as different and unequal places of liturgical action. This approach does not exclude participation by other members of the congregation, but it is the actions and words of the priest that are most important for liturgical effectiveness.

In contrast to the priestly approach, a 'popular' approach is concerned mainly with how the liturgy attracts and communicates immediately to everyone, even those who are not yet members of the Christian community. Its symbols (its language, its music, its dress, its appeal to contemporary motivations) therefore derive as much as possible from the culture of the congregation but especially from contemporary popular culture as presented in popular music and video/film. It aims for relevance rather than traditional symbolism; it diminishes the symbols of the sacred; it expects an engaging performance from its leaders; its liturgy is adaptable and informal. A popular approach thus encourages congregational activity controlled by a charismatic leader and popular music rather than by established liturgical rules.

The two approaches described above are stereotypes. They describe the two ends of a spectrum. One emphasizes the role of the ordained priest, the other emphasizes the contemporary relevance of liturgy. They do both include some kind of participation by the community in addition to that of the designated leaders. Both need and hope for an active congregational involvement. But neither of them is particularly focused on active participation as its main theme. This book, on the other hand, is particularly focused on the theme of active participation.

Who wrote this book and why?

Neil Darragh is the writer of this book. But he has not written it alone. It has been written with the collaboration of many liturgical ministers and planners, colleagues and students. In particular it has been written in collaboration with Jo Ayers. Jo contributed to several of the chapters in their initial stage and has acted as editor and critic of the book in its final stage. Both Neil and Jo have had extensive experience of Eucharists where there has been high participation. They have also experienced Eucharists in which nearly everyone except the presider was reduced to passivity. Both have taught liturgics and liturgical theology at tertiary level and in local parish ministry training. Both have also been members for many years of liturgical committees that plan liturgies at the local community level. Jo's contribution to liturgical renewal derives from her reflections as a lay woman with extensive ministry experience in Eucharist and as a marriage and funeral celebrant. Neil draws on the experience of a diocesan priest as a liturgical leader and as one who has also spent time sitting in the pews in the course of liturgical research.

We have a shared conviction out of our own experience and research that *high active participation in Eucharist enriches the symbolism of Eucharist and enhances its impact on people's lives.* Sunday Eucharists dominated by a single priest presider impoverish that symbolism. Different cultures have different expectations about participation in church and society. Underlying this book is a culture that values participation in church and society and believes in the added value that teamwork and inclusiveness bring to human relationships and common enterprises.

We also have a conviction that high active participation can be fairly easily achieved by local communities, provided their liturgical planners and ministers see this as an important goal; provided too that they have some guiding principles to help them actually do it. Often local communities, including their priests, see their goal as simply to embellish and adapt a little what is laid down in the official books[2]. In that case there is little to be gained from reading this book.

If, on the other hand, local liturgical planners accept that they, as well as and perhaps more than the official liturgical books and rubrics, are responsible for the impact their Sunday Eucharists have on their own people, they are then set for a real engagement of liturgy and life. It is not a matter here of exposing Sunday Eucharists to the individual fantasies of local liturgists. Most communities want empowering rather than simply chaotic or whimsical or radical results from their liturgical planners. This book proposes perspectives and principles that we believe will lead liturgical planners towards high active participation of people in Sunday Eucharists.

Who is the book written for?

Priests, ministers, and liturgical planners in local communities such as parishes or chaplaincies are the main people we have in mind in writing this book. We use the term 'liturgical planners and ministers' as a general term to include all those who have a deliberate influence on what happens in the local Sunday Eucharist. Among these a key role is that of the priest whose attitude to participation may, more than any other, make the difference between success and failure. Some of what happens in Eucharist is the work of a liturgy committee who plan the liturgy beforehand. But some of it is also the work of liturgical ministers on the spot who may or may not have been part of an earlier planning group.

In addressing this book to liturgical planners and ministers, we have in mind people who have some experience of how liturgy works at a practical level, who have a sensitivity to what good and bad liturgy looks and feels like, and who are used to feedback from the local community. We hope also

---

2. The issue of the interpretation of liturgical laws is one that liturgical planners often face. Current discussion of liturgical law and its interpretation is complex for the non-lawyer, but in any case it is a matter of interpretation not simply 'obedience'. Some recent articles that deal helpfully with this issue are R. Kevin Seasoltz, "Liturgy and Ecclesiastical Law: Some Canonical and Pastoral Challenges," *Worship* 85, no. 6 (2011): 520-41; and Jan R. Larson, "A Case for Changing Liturgical Words," *Worship* 86, no. 1 (2012): 60-70.

that among the readers will be people who have more extensive experience or extended study of liturgy. Such people will be able to interpret the more unusual or more difficult parts of this book to others.

The book is addressed primarily to Catholic communities of the Roman Rite. At one point, because of our involvement and collaboration with liturgists of other churches, we envisaged a book that could encompass the range of Eucharists across the main Christian denominations. This probably could have been achieved if the book had been pitched at a higher level discussion of the theology or history of Eucharist[3]. Many of the contemporary challenges at the level of hands-on liturgical planning however are specific to one church rather than another.

There are specific challenges to local liturgies which derive from the Roman Rite that do not occur in other Rites or in other church denominations. And churches that celebrate Eucharist without official texts and rubrics face a very different set of challenges. Although the principles of liturgical participation we discuss here have wide application across the mainstream Christian churches, the examples and the issues we deal with derive specifically from the Roman Rite[4].

The process of liturgical change

Liturgical change is a process rather than a product of planning. *It is more important that liturgical planners get the process right than that they produce the perfect liturgy at any particular time.* Liturgical planners sit at the interface of their own local community and the liturgical books that contain the words and rules for celebrating Eucharist. It is relatively easy to access the official liturgical books. It is much more difficult to maintain the ongoing relationships with a diverse and often changing local community. An essen-

---

3. Contemporary lines of both liturgical convergence and divergence are described and illustrated in presentations from a wide range of Christian churches and communities in Thomas F. Best and Dagmar Heller, eds., *Worship Today: Understanding, Practice, Ecumenical Implications* (Geneva: WCC Publications, 2004).
4. For a detailed and critical examination of the current state of official Eucharist texts of the Roman Rite, readers may consult Edward Foley, Nathan D. Mitchell, and Joanne Pierce, eds., *A Commentary on the General Instruction of the Roman Missal* (Collegeville, MN: Liturgical Press, 2007). For readers who require something less substantial and more concise but that still gives a sense of what is happening here, there is a brief summary and review of this commentary in John M. Huels, "A Commentary on the General Instruction of the Roman Missal," *Worship* 82, no. 5 (2008): 433-45.

tial ingredient of good liturgical planning is the ongoing conversation and negotiation that planners and ministers maintain with the rest of the local community.

Liturgy planners often occupy a difficult position. They may want to promote particular changes and be able to give good theological reasons for why these changes should take place, but face opposition from other members of the community. All the issues addressed in this book and all the solutions proposed here assume that liturgical planners are involved in a process of communication and negotiation within their local communities. Liturgical change is sometimes slow. It gets faster when the planners are trusted by the community.

Successful change and successful maintenance are built on relationships of trust which are established over time. Even one unilateral decision by a local priest, for example, may severely damage people's commitment to participation. *Community members need to be sure that they will not be bullied, that their expectations of liturgy will be respected, that stimulation to change will take place within agreed boundaries and with explanations, that their feedback will be taken into account, and that liturgical changes can be reversed.* Without this kind of trust, liturgical change will become an exercise in power rather than in creative communication. Its results may be the opposite of that intended by the planners—conflict and division rather than Eucharist.

All the suggestions for enhanced participation in Eucharist contained in this book are proposed on the assumption that liturgical planners and ministers already have and intend to maintain this relationship of trust with their communities. Evaluations of liturgy in the community need to be regular, representative, and honest. Nothing replaces the continuing conversations among members of the community where people come to understand one another's spirituality and theological world view. The way these conversations take place will differ in each local community according to its own makeup of cultures, age-groups, socio-economic levels, educational background, and theological perspectives.

The primary responsibility of liturgical planners and ministers is to understand how these conversations work and to value them. Without this, any attempt at changing liturgical symbols is self-defeating. We hope this book will feed into those conversations.

Considerations of liturgical space

A Sunday Eucharist occurs at a particular time and place. The 'time' in which Sunday Eucharist takes place is the subject of a later chapter dedicated to the liturgical calendar. The 'place' of Sunday Eucharist includes the environmental, architectural and artistic features of the building with its own internal arrangement of space. Liturgical planners often wish the place were different—that the seating could be rearranged, that the sanctuary was higher or lower or broader, that the aisles were wider, that the gathering space was bigger, that the visual art was more aesthetic, or that we could build a completely new church.

We know the arrangements of the space within which a Sunday Eucharist takes place, along with the visual art displayed there, are among the most powerful determinants of what will happen there—the way people relate to one another, the distinctions between sacred and ordinary, the organization of ministry, the effectiveness of sound, the possibilities for liturgical movement, and the sense of celebration and community. But liturgical planners and ministers seldom, perhaps only once or twice in a lifetime, get a chance to change them. For this reason we have not given dedicated attention to them in this book that is focused on the weekly liturgical decisions of liturgical planners.

We hope though that readers interested in the topics of art and architecture might follow through with other reading elsewhere. Liturgical space is now a controversial topic of increasing importance because contemporary liturgy does not always fit well in older churches and because of the large number of new churches recently built or under construction[5].

---

5. For a substantial overview of Christian architecture and art from early Christianity to the present, see R. Kevin Seasoltz, *A Sense of the Sacred: Theological Foundations of Christian Architecture and Art* (New York / London: Continuum, 2008). Or for a much briefer overview by the same author, see "Sacred Space, the Arts and Theology: Some Light from History," *Worship* 82, no. 6 (2008): 519-42. For an examination of liturgical space, both Catholic and Protestant, in reformation and post-reformation Western Europe, see Nigel Yates, *Liturgical Space: Christian Worship and Church Buildings in Western Europe 1500 - 2000* (Hampshire: Ashgate, 2008). A recent study of a sample of ten Protestant, Orthodox, and Catholic congregations in Southern California that argues for the relevance and persistence of imaginative traditions in art is William A. Dyrness, *Senses of the Soul: Art and the Visual in Christian Worship* (Eugene, Oregon: Cascade Books, 2008). An article that addresses the more basic question of how to interpret liturgical space is Mark E. Wedig, "No Neutral Zones: Hermeneutics and the Interpretation of Liturgical Space," *Liturgical Ministry* 14, Winter (2005): 1-7. And for a more contentious argument against 'modernist' architecture and in favour of a more transcendental liturgical space outside or at one end of the church, see Moyra Doorly, *No Place for God: The Denial of the Transcendent in Modern Church Architecture* (San Francisco: Ignatius Press, 2007).

How should liturgical planners and ministers use this book?

The chapters of this book are best read in sequence since nearly all aspects of the Eucharist liturgy are interrelated. The practicalities of liturgical planning often mean however that something brief and focused is what is required at a particular time. We have attempted therefore to construct the chapters as much as possible so that liturgical planners and ministers may be able to read the particular chapter on a topic that concerns them at a particular time without having to have read the whole book. This has meant some repetition, usually brief, across chapters.

The first paragraph of each chapter sets out briefly the topic dealt with in that chapter. At the end of the chapter is a list of questions which reflect the main challenges that we sought to deal with in that chapter. These questions may also serve as discussion questions for group sessions or a way for the readers to review what they have understood from the chapter.

We hope too that liturgy committees or in-service training sessions for ministers may be able to read and discuss the particular chapters that concern them. Nevertheless we have also tried to avoid too much repetition from one chapter to another with the result that most chapters do to some extent still rely on one another. It will help then if there are at least some people in the group who have read the whole book and can indicate where matters of interest are discussed in other chapters.

Although we have tried to maintain some relative independence among chapters, there is nevertheless a momentum to the book that carries through from the first to the last chapter.

The first two chapters (*Chapter 1: Active Participation* and *Chapter 2: The Current Context*) address the basic questions that flow through the whole book. These are firstly what we mean by, what we see as the features of, 'active participation'. Secondly, they are to do with the wider historical and ritual context we need to take into account for active participation to be achievable.

There follows a chapter (*Chapter 3: The Christian Assembly and its Ministries*) on the ways people participate in the assembly that gathers for Eucharist. This chapter focuses especially on the liturgical ministers who are a major component of active participation.

The following three chapters (*Chapter 4: The Rites of Gathering and Sending, Chapter 5: The Liturgy of the Word,* and *Chapter 6: The Liturgy of Eucharist*) describe in turn the possibilities for active participation in each of the major 'phases' of the Eucharist liturgy.

Leadership and music are two important components of Eucharist that are not easily discussed within the 'phases' of the liturgy since they run through all of them. We have addressed these in separate chapters (*Chapter 7: Leadership* and *Chapter 8: Music*).

The following two chapters (*Chapter 9: The Calendar* and *Chapter 10: Related Liturgies*) are concerned with two larger contexts with which the weekly Sunday Eucharist interacts. These are the recurring cycles of time represented by the liturgical calendar, and the various liturgies other than Sunday Eucharists which are also part of the liturgical life of the local community.

A final chapter (*Chapter 11: Eucharist in the local church*) is addressed to the more basic question of how we see our role as local planners and ministers. It is concerned with a theme that underlies all the previous chapters, namely, our understanding of local church and how this understanding influences the way we celebrate our Sunday Eucharists.

The use of endnotes

Throughout this book we have used endnotes in a particular way. We have assumed that most readers will be interested in the implications of this book for their own local Eucharists rather than in its relationship to the wider liturgical literature. There may however be some readers who wish to follow up on particular points. It is for these latter readers that we have added the endnotes which are effectively 'further reading'.

For the most part these further readings are chosen for their readability in the sense that they are both written in accessible English and of direct contemporary interest (rather than background information) for liturgical ministry. We have occasionally included some of this 'background' type reading where it seemed particularly helpful to do so. Occasionally too we have used the endnotes to give necessary acknowledgements of ideas or quotations from other writings. On the whole though, the endnotes may be regarded simply as suggested further reading for those wishing to follow up on a particular interest.

Chapter 1
Active Participation

The central theme of this book is active participation in Eucharist. In this chapter we note some of the different ways in which people talk about participation. We set out three key features that mark a high level of active participation in Eucharist, namely a Eucharist that is hospitable, inclusive, and outgoing.

What kind of participation?

Very few people involved in liturgy today are actually against participation as such. There are different views though on what kind or what level of participation is desirable. These different views are not just interesting points for discussion but lead to remarkably different kinds of liturgy.

One understanding of participation, for example, is that the congregation engages in uniform responses to the liturgical leader and in combined recital of the specifically congregational parts of the Eucharist. Hopefully these would be wholehearted responses by the whole congregation, would be beautifully sung with musical accompaniment, and sometimes interspersed with choir or solo singing. There is undoubted power, beauty, and a sense of belonging in such participation when it works fully and well. When it fails, whether from lack of skill or from congregational disinterest, it is dull and dispiriting. In the worst case, the congregation are barely participants but have become uniform respondents.

As well as simple failure, this kind of participation also has the potential for its own particular aberrations. Examples of these are the choir 'takeover' that excludes the rest of the congregation, the mechanical recital in unison of the people's responses, or the manipulated crowd response in the style of a live television show. The fact that many of us have encountered such failures does not mean we should dismiss the power of this kind of participation by uniform response when it is performed fully and well.

There is another kind of participation where the majority of the congregation are mainly silent and might appear to be passive but are actively intent on the words and actions of the liturgy. The participation in this case is one of listening and observing. It may engage the congregation mentally and emotionally even though they make no obvious contribution to the liturgical action. This is sometimes described as 'interior' participation. There are people, times, and places where this kind of participation carries a silent intensity of interior but communal prayer and a sense of mystery. But again, it can fail. It can become a silent endurance with liturgical leaders performing almost magical rites from which the congregation hopes to obtain some merit.

This kind of participation in Eucharist also has its own potential aberrations. Examples of this are when the priest appears to be simply going about his own business ignoring the congregation; or conversely, when the members of the congregation are intent on their own business or reciting their own prayers—only their presence is required, not their attention. Again, although we may have sometimes encountered it in its failed forms, this kind of participation by silent attention has a recognizable energy and the liturgical symbols themselves can lead participants into this interior awareness.[1]

We have considered these two understandings of participation because some modified form of them is often proposed in practical discussions on liturgical planning and performance. Neither of them is exactly what we mean by participation in this book, but they are important in that they are valuable *ingredients* of what we understand here as full participation. Even when they are not ingredients in a fuller participation, they may still be important in some circumstance and places and for some people. There are occasions or communities where communal responses are all that is needed. There are occasions when a silent but intense and attentive participation in Eucharist is called for. There need not be just one meaning of participation that suits everybody all the time. Nevertheless the active participation in Sunday Eu-

---

1. What has been variously called the contemplative Mass, the silent Eucharist, or the Buddhist liturgy that is characterized by God-awareness is described in Aloysius Pieris, 'An Asian Way to Celebrate the Eucharist', in *Worship* 81/4 (2007): 314–28. This kind of liturgy need not be specifically Asian and is currently practised in a variety of cultures, usually in small groups. An argument for more interior participation that derives from active involvement in the ritual action rather than competing with it is proposed in Donald G LaSalle, 'Participation: The Heart of Eucharistic Devotion', in *Liturgical Ministry* 16, Winter (2007): 19–29.

charists that is the aim of this book is one that is fuller than the two kinds described above.[2]

Key features of active participation

Active participation in Eucharist as we envisage it is liturgical action that is *hospitable, inclusive,* and *outgoing*. We may regard these as three 'features' of liturgy that we can aim for in liturgical planning so as to achieve high active participation. These features overlap to some extent but each of them highlights some aspect of active participation that needs the attention of liturgical planners and ministers.[3]

An important element in building active participation in Eucharist is the recognition that the impact of liturgical actions may differ between one community and another. *Symbolic actions may have a different meaning and therefore a different impact depending on the mixture of cultures and traditions that make up the local community.* The way in which hospitality is expressed, for example, will differ according to the culturally different ways of extending hospitality in the wider society. The way in which active participation is hospitable, inclusive and outgoing in actual practice will require therefore sensitivity to cultural and traditional diversity within local Christian communities.

Hospitable

A Eucharist is most obviously *hospitable* when there is a sense of welcome to all potential participants. This sense of being welcome should include the

---

2. The Second Vatican Council's Constitution on the Liturgy encourages *full, conscious,* and *active participation* in the liturgy (*Sacrosanctum Concilium*, 24). For a fairly detailed study of the origins and implications of each of these terms, the reader may usefully consult Martin Stuflesser, '*Actuosa Participatio*: Between Hectic Actionism and New Interiority. Reflections On "Active Participation" In the Worship of the Church as Both Right and Obligation of the Faithful', *Studia Liturgica* 41/1 (2011): 92–126.
3. For the sake of comparison, readers may wish to consult the different but compatible description of active participation as performative, self-engaging, aesthetic and evocative in Vivian Ligo, 'Liturgy as Enactment', in *Worship* 83/5 (2009): 398–414. Again by way of comparison, an ecumenical book, written by a Jewish writer for worship committees in churches and synagogues, has a similar intention of empowering lay people and clergy to work together. Here a worship service is assessed by its evidence of pastoral care, of prophetic commitment, and of priestly invocation of the presence of God. See Lawrence A Hoffman, *The Art of Public Prayer: Not for Clergy Only* (Woodstock, Vermont: Skylight Paths Publishing, second edition, 1999).

community's own members, for even longstanding members can come to feel marginal or unappreciated if they are ignored. The welcome similarly extends to returning members who for whatever reason have not been part of the community's Eucharists for some time. Most importantly it extends to newcomers, travellers and seekers.

The Eucharist of a local community such as a parish is hospitable, and in that sense has high active participation, when it is successful in including in some manner all the variety of people who make up that particular locality. Such a local community would seek to be open in its membership, in its liturgical symbols, and especially in its decision-making to all the variety of cultural, ethnic, language, age-group, gender, socio-economic and environmental characteristics of the locality.

Hospitality as a feature of active participation in Eucharist is an ongoing project that requires continuing adjustment of liturgical symbols such as languages used, gesture and posture, styles of movement, dress, and recruitment of ministers as the make-up of the local community changes over time. It is a process in which Eucharist adjusts to and incorporates changes in the local community that occur, for example, through changes in ethnic migration, new housing, population changes and environmental shifts.

Being hospitable is not however just about those *to whom* hospitality is offered. It is also about those *by whom* the hospitality is offered. A less discussed aspect of being hospitable is the nature of the host place and host community. There are already established characteristics of any home-place where Eucharist is celebrated. One important characteristic, for example, is that the host community is Christian, and since we are concerned specifically here with the Roman Rite, that it is Catholic. Those who belong in that host community need to be sensitive and welcoming to newcomers. But they are also the guardians of their own communal identity. Over the years the host community will have developed its own communal style of being Christian—an emphasis perhaps on social justice, or care for children, or environmental concern, or respect for the elderly, or a particular cultural emphasis, or some combinations of all of these. Their liturgical symbols will express this.

By being open and welcoming, the hosts, those who have already established this home-place, do not abandon their own home to the whims of passers-by or to whatever the newcomers may require of them. Those who are newcomers are asked to be sensitive to the nature of the liturgical home that has already been created here. At the same time the host community is challenged to examine whether it has become too set in its ways or too narrow in its vision.

Being the guardians of the home identity is a process of change not merely a conservation of the past. All of this, the home identity and the constantly changing needs of hospitality to newcomers, needs to be signalled in the liturgical actions of Eucharist. All members of that community bear responsibility for creating this hospitable atmosphere, but it is particularly the actions and words of the ministers and leaders who will do this more than others. Just how the symbols of Eucharist do this and can be adjusted to do it better is a matter we will address in later chapters of this book.

In fact, strictly local communities are often incapable of being hospitable to everyone. They may need to be complemented by more specialised Eucharists at a wider regional level such as a diocese. There are Eucharists which are not 'local' in the sense that they are not identified by neighbourhood, suburb, or town but cater for specialist communities such as a particular ethnic or language group, or households of vowed religious, or the deaf community, or a school community. The task here for liturgical planners is to ensure that local community Eucharists and the Eucharists of such specialised communities work in a complementary way rather than in competition with one another. Here the local Eucharistic community can recognise the value of its own belonging to and participation in the wider level of diocesan planning.

Ultimately it is the hospitality of the Creator that is at stake here. A Eucharistic community can be hospitable if it has a deep sense that it is participating in the hospitality of God who created this place long ago and continues to be the welcoming host to this contemporary community. The liturgical actions of Eucharist engage the Christian people in the interplays of people and place within God's hospitality. The hospitality of God is the process in which this community's identity as both home-people and pilgrim-people is being created.[4]

Inclusive

We use the term *inclusive* here to characterize a Eucharist that includes active participation of many of its participants, rather than just a restricted few, in its internal ministries and liturgical action. While hospitality is the outward face of the community to the wider locality, inclusiveness (as we use the term

---

4. For more on liturgical hospitality, see Frank Coady, 'Hospitality in Liturgy', in *Liturgical Ministry* 11, Fall (2002): 182–86. See also the booklet addressed to a mainly Anglican readership that argues for a more accessible liturgy, Mark Earey and Carolyn Headley, *Mission and Liturgical Worship* (Cambridge, England: Grove Books, 2002).

here) is the inward face of the community looking at its own internal relationships.

At its most general level, liturgical planners are ensuring that their Eucharists are inclusive when the liturgical words and actions are gender-inclusive, culture-inclusive, age-inclusive and socio-economically varied. Put negatively this means that liturgical planners are careful they are not somehow, even unintentionally, excluding people from active participation because of such things as gender, ethnicity, language or age.

An inclusive Eucharist goes further than the participation by communal responses and silent attention noted earlier in this chapter. Eucharists are inclusive in this internal sense when they are the result of wide participation in decisions on the incorporation of cultural symbols, gender-inclusive language, age-related music, and so on in the Eucharist. Put negatively, if liturgy is always done by the same person or persons, if only men or the elderly have ministerial roles in the Eucharist, or if the cultural symbols of only one ethnic group appear there, or if the language appears to imply that the congregation are all male or that God is male, then the Eucharists of that community are exclusive in these senses. They reduce the possibilities of active participation or may even be discriminatory. Most decisively, Eucharists are inclusive when many and varied members of the congregation actively participate in the ministries that make up the Eucharist.

Because the term 'inclusive' is sometimes used to imply that there are no boundaries or criteria at all, it may help here to approach this issue from the negative side, that is, to state what inclusiveness is not. Firstly, it does not mean that every member of the community has to participate equally in every action of the liturgy regardless of their own prior personal, cultural or ecclesial experience. We might decide, for example, that gender is not a relevant criterion for deciding who should or should not be readers at Eucharist. At the same time we might well decide that an ability to read Scripture clearly and meaningfully in public is indeed a requirement for the role of reader. In this case, gender is not a criterion for inclusion or exclusion, but reading skill is.

Secondly, liturgical inclusiveness is not a matter of 'everyone gets a turn'. Such a principle would be automatically exclusive since not everyone wants 'a turn' and will go elsewhere to avoid such a regime. The modification 'everyone who wants to gets a turn' produces its own problems of self-selection and unskilful performance well known to liturgical planners.

Being inclusive liturgically is not then about treating everyone the same and ignoring talents, lifestyle, and culture. It is a discerning inclusiveness that acknowledges a variety of gifts for the building up of the community. We give more responsibility to some people rather than others. We recognise the gifts that belong to some people rather than others. We acknowledge the kind of witness inherent in some people's lives but not in others. These discernments recognise variety among people and different kinds of suitability for ministry. From these come the criteria for finding the people who can provide the service required by each particular ministry.

The community will need a process for deciding upon and administering such criteria and for seeing that people are not excluded by *irrelevant* criteria. A liturgy that is conducted almost entirely by one or two ordained ministers, for example, is one that fails to be inclusive and lacks this key feature of active participation.

Put briefly, a Eucharist may be regarded as inclusive in the sense used in this book when its words and actions are gender-inclusive, culture-inclusive, age-inclusive, includes socio-economic variety, recognisably employs the symbols of the people, and when it includes the gifts, skills, and witness of its members in its liturgical ministries.

Outgoing

A third key feature of active participation in Eucharist is its *outgoing* or missionary energy that sends the participants out into world as participants in God's reign in the world. Why do you, or why should anyone for that matter, take part in the Eucharist? And for what reason would anyone want to be there regularly and often? What is the Eucharist *for*? Some people have answered this by saying that it is not *for* anything. It is worshipping God which is inherent in the nature of human beings and human communities. It is an end in itself, and to ask what it is for is to reduce it to a utility, an instrument we use to achieve something else.

Other people have commonly regarded Eucharist as a means to spiritual growth. In this case it can variously be understood as a point of access to God's grace, a source of God's compassion, a humanly rewarding encounter with the divine, an encouragement and renewal on the way to being Christ's disciples, a renewal of the Holy Spirit within.

All of these views point to the Eucharist as resourcing human life and indicate that this is what it is for. Some would accent the personal gains to be had there; others would accent the community building that occurs there. The phrase from the Second Vatican Council that describes Eucharist as both the 'summit' and the 'source' of the church's life (*Constitution on the*

Sacred Liturgy, No 10) serves to bring together the dual focus of Eucharist. It says that Eucharist is both the summit, that is, the goal towards which Christian life tends, but also the source, that is, a means to living fully the Christian life beyond and outside of Eucharist. In this latter dimension it is outgoing or missionary.

This outgoing feature of Eucharist is concerned with the Eucharist as a means or resource *for* something else. That 'something else' can be summed up as participating in bringing about God's reign in the world. This outgoing or missionary quality of the Eucharist is that it is *for* the transformation of the world in which we live.[5] It is not just about transforming the people who are liturgical participants. Active participation in Eucharist includes this sense of missionary energy that reaches out from Eucharist and into the world beyond Eucharist. This is not just a generalised recognition that the Christian community is always involved in God's mission. It is made particular and concrete in the words and actions of each Eucharist.

The liturgical symbols, especially the words and actions of the ministers, engage the participants in this missionary outreach when they constantly point towards this larger participation in God's mission for the wider world.

---

5. This feature of participation in Eucharist as missionary or outgoing is one that may be less familiar to liturgical planners. It is a feature that has received a good deal of attention in recent writings on Eucharist. A reader-friendly, mainstream presentation of this missionary feature of Eucharist is given in Gregory F Augustine Pierce, *The Mass Is Never Ended: Rediscovering Our Mission to Transform the World* (Notre Dame, Indiana: Ave Maria Press, 2007). At a more theological but still easily accessible level, see Patrick T McCormick, *A Banqueter's Guide to the All-Night Soup Kitchen of the Kingdom of God* (Collegeville, Minnesota: Liturgical Press, 2004). See also the treatment of the morality of Eucharist in Joseph Martos, *The Sacraments: An Interdisciplinary and Interactive Study* (Collegeville, Minnesota: Liturgical Press, 2009). Also at a more theological level, see David N Power, 'The Eucharistic Table: In Communion with the Hungry', in *Worship* 83/5 (2009): 386–98. A book that makes the connection between Eucharist and justice by focusing on several 'moments' in the Eucharistic texts is Margaret Scott, *The Eucharist and Social Justice* (New York/Mahwah, NJ: Paulist Press, 2009). An article that summarizes some recent writing on the link between Eucharist and mission and proposes self-emptying humility, radical inclusivity, and prophetic service as the three characteristics for Eucharist as liturgy and as mission is Gloria L Schaab, '"As Christ, So We": Eucharist as Liturgy', in *Liturgical Ministry* 18, Fall (2009): 171–81.

As well as outreach to social justice in the world, more attention is also being given today to the outreach of Eucharist towards the wider creation, that is, to ecological issues. Several journal articles deal with liturgy and ecology in 'Green Liturgy', in *Liturgical Ministry* 20, Spring (2011): 57–95.

The most obvious place where this is done symbolically is in the Sending Rite at the end where the announcements, prayers, and blessing can state explicitly what people are being sent out for from this particular Eucharist.

This sense of outreach needs also to be there interwoven through or permeating the whole liturgy. Prayers of intercession, for example, that show a concern for the wider world, notices that invite engagement in social concerns, interpretations of Scripture that are conscious of society and environment, and awareness of the public engagements of members of the community all point the assembly towards what the Eucharist is for. As we are sent back into the world we go with a sense of mission to the world.

Where this is not the case, active participation is truncated. It is reduced to participation in the liturgy itself rather than to participation in its mission. Active participation implies that the liturgical symbols of Eucharist engage the participants not just in the community's gathering for Eucharist but also in the community's outreach beyond Eucharist. Ultimately, it is God's mission in the world that is the foundation for Eucharist. Eucharist empowers its participants into becoming active in that larger mission.

Conclusion

This chapter has sought to explain one of the foundational ideas of this book, namely, an active participation in Eucharist that is hospitable, inclusive and outgoing. This understanding of active participation in Eucharist provides us with a basic orientation that can guide our liturgical planning and performance of ministry in local communities.

Key questions:

1) What are the key features of active participation in Eucharist? What is our own best experience of these in action?
2) To whom should the liturgy be hospitable, and what are the responsibilities of the hosts?
3) In what sense can the Eucharist liturgy be inclusive or exclusive of its own participants?
4) What is implied in saying that Eucharist is outgoing, and how does the liturgy normally symbolise this missionary outreach?
5) When we consider the Eucharist in which we normally participate, what is done well to achieve a hospitable, inclusive and outgoing liturgy? What could be improved?

Chapter 2
The Current Context

The central theme of this book, as outlined in the previous chapter, is active participation in Eucharist that is hospitable, inclusive, and outgoing. That theme focuses the aims of liturgical planning and ministry. This second chapter is about *the context within which* we set out to achieve such active participation. This context is not primarily something that we set out to change. It is more like the set of existing realities within which we will have to work—not necessarily unchangeable, but not our focus of attention either. These are the 'givens' so to speak that we will normally have to work within. If we ignore these or if we get these wrong, we are unlikely to succeed in our primary aim. They are not the meal on the table; they are the table and the dishes that hold the meal ready for us to eat.

We propose to examine here two main facets of this context. The first of these is *historical*. The theme of active participation has become important liturgically because of the particular period in the history of the Christian church in which we now live. The second of these is to do with the nature of Eucharist as *ritual*. Eucharist is a kind of ritual with its own 'rules' of interaction. If we don't know about them or ignore them, our good intentions in liturgical planning may result in something quite different from what we hoped for.

The historical context

In what ways is the historical context important to our project? In the early decades of the twenty-first century we have reached a crossroads in liturgical understanding and practice. This is the second such crossroads that the Christian community has encountered within the memory of its older members.

The first crossroads in living memory was reached in the early 1970s when most of the churches in the Western European tradition made significant changes in their patterns of worship.¹ This renewal was fuelled by research into early Christian liturgical traditions and by a concern that liturgy communicate better with contemporary generations. This resulted in major revisions of the official or semi-official liturgical books of many churches during the 1970s.

Such an extensive renewal of major rituals was not peculiar to churches. It was paralleled, for example, at almost exactly the same time by an official renewal of public ritual in the Soviet Union. Like the renewal of the Roman Rite, the Soviet renewal was centrally controlled from the mid-1960s.² Renewals of major rituals are not always successful in meeting the hopes of the planners. We know now in hindsight that the Soviet renewal of state ritual had faltered, then collapsed, by the end of the 1980s along with the regime it was intended to support. There are no guarantees that the renewal of church rituals will not follow a similar path.

The twenty-first century–the second crossroads

At this time in the twenty-first century we are standing again hesitantly at a second crossroads.³ Today local liturgical planners may find themselves caught in disagreements that are not just about how to do things on Sunday

---

1. For readers interested in the larger historical picture, James F White describes Catholic worship between the Council of Trent and the Second Vatican Council (essentially between 1563 and 1963) as part of the social and cultural shifts in Europe and North America in *Roman Catholic Worship: Trent to Today* (Collegeville, Minnesota: Liturgical Press, 2003). Liturgical movements across denominational lines over the last hundred years or so and the visions that underlie them are summarised in Frank C Senn, 'Four Liturgical Movements: Restoration, Renewal, Revival, Retrieval', in *Liturgy* 19/4 (2004): 69–79. And for a brief interpretation of the antagonistic 'strands' that led into and continued through Vatican II, see Gavin Brown, 'From Stages to Strands: Re-Interpreting the Liturgical Movement', in *Pacifica* 23/1 (2010): 58–83.
2. There is a description and analysis of this renewal in some detail in Christel Lane, *The Rites of Rulers: Ritual in Industrial Society—the Soviet Case* (Cambridge: Cambridge University Press, 1981), see especially 54.
3. Readers may get a good sense of the transition and crises affecting liturgy in the first decade of the twenty-first century especially in the United States by reading the several articles in 'Liturgy's Crises', *Liturgical Ministry* 17, Winter (2008). For a readable but well documented discussion of the historical lead-up to what we describe here as the 'second crossroads', see Rita Ferrone, *Liturgy: Sacrosanctum Concilium*, Rediscovering Vatican II (New York/Mahwah: Paulist Press, 2007). And for a brief survey of Roman liturgical reforms since Vatican II, see Keith F Pecklers, '40 Years of Liturgical Reform: Shaping Roman Catholic Worship for the 21st Century', in *Worship* 79/3 (2005): 194–208. Or for

but clearly reflect more fundamental differences on how to deal with liturgical change. Some people, for example, advocate doing only what is required or permitted in the official documents. Others regret the liturgical reforms of Vatican II or think they have gone too far and support liturgical change only if it is a return to earlier forms of the Eucharist liturgy. Others wish to advance the official reforms in the direction they have taken since Vatican II and so support pushing the boundaries of permissible adaptations. Others advocate more inculturation of the Eucharist liturgy and therefore also more diversity in liturgical actions.

While liturgical planners may encounter any or all of these viewpoints, it may be helpful in local communities to see these various viewpoints as falling into two broad currents. One current includes those who hold that much of the renewal of liturgy has now faltered or gone astray or was a mistake in the first place and seeks a 'restoration' of the substance of the historic liturgies by means of centralized church planning. A second current, by contrast, regards the 'renewal' of liturgy as still ongoing and requiring attention in particular to the many contemporary cultures in which liturgy is celebrated.[4]

We should be careful in discussing these currents of restoration and renewal not to see them as alternatives. There is common ground, but there are differences of emphasis and these will result in different liturgical choices. In the 1970s there were restorationist and renewal currents that fed into and energized one another. In the 2010s there is a danger often confronted in liturgy committees that, instead of feeding into one another, the restorationist and renewal currents may separate into two streams unintelligible to each other.

---

a more substantial and detailed discussion focused on the new Roman Missal, see the same author's *The Ethos of the Roman Rite: On the Reception and Implementation of the New Missal* (London/Collegeville, MN: Continuum/Liturgical Press, 2009). For a sense of what this book says in a more succinct package, readers may prefer the summary and critique in R Kevin Seasoltz, 'The Genius of the Roman Rite: On the Reception and Implementation of the New Missal', in *Worship* 83/6 (2009): 541–50.

Since our attitudes to recent historical change depend a good deal on how we think it all started in the first century, readers may be interested in the wider than usual examination of the origins of Eucharist in Andrew McGowan, 'Rethinking Eucharistic Origins', in *Pacifica* 23/2 (2010): 173–91.

4. A brief and accessible argument for diversity rather than uniformity based on Vatican II's *Constitution on the Liturgy* and other official documents is proposed in Nathan D Mitchell, "The Amen Corner', in *Worship* 77/2 (2003): 171–81. For a passionate and well argued critique of the restorationist position, see John Hill, 'Can Restorationism Succeed?'', in *The Australasian Catholic Record* 86/3 (2009): 259–76.

This historical context often puts liturgical planners and ministers in situations where they are aware among themselves of differences of approach to liturgy, but are not sure of the basis for such differences. One important basis for such differences lies in attitudes to *unity* and *diversity*.

A key issue concerning the *unity* of the church as expressed in liturgy is, How do we celebrate Eucharist in a way that clearly expresses the unity of the local community (the community that assembles for Sunday Eucharist) with the many other such communities that make up the wider church? It is perhaps easiest to illustrate the issue here by describing what the two extreme responses would look like. One extreme would say there is no 'wider' church. The community that assembles on Sundays has its own leaders and makes its own best decisions without needing to be too concerned about the wider church. The other extreme would maintain that it is the 'universal' church that is the body of Christ. Every celebration of Eucharist is then an embodiment of that universal church and, in order that this be evident at every time and place, the celebration of Eucharist should be decided not by the local community but by the central authority of the church.

This book assumes that the liturgical planners and ministers to whom it is addressed will want to seek some middle ground between these two extremes, that is, they will exercise some decision-making about their liturgy at the local level, but will want to do so in a manner that retains a dynamic unity, not necessarily a uniformity, within the wider church.

There are two kinds of *diversity* that are most likely to concern liturgical planners and ministers. These are *cultural* diversity and *generational* diversity. The kind of cultural diversity that is most likely to affect us at the level of Sunday Eucharist, is the cultural diversity that now exists *within* many local communities. Many Eucharists are now celebrated by culturally diverse participants. Attention to cultural diversity has made us conscious that the historic liturgies of the major Rites, such as the Roman Rite, the Coptic Rite, or the Syro-Malabar Rite, are liturgies created out of particular cultural contexts in the past.

These ancient liturgies are the result of the inculturation of liturgy in the cultures of the past. They now constitute part of our historic Christian identity. They have also set the precedent for the continuing inculturation of liturgy today. A central task of liturgical planners and ministers today is to maintain identity with an historic rite such as the Roman Rite but in interaction with the diversity of cultures that make up their contemporary Christian community.

The diversity between *generations* is a second major kind of diversity that concerns liturgical planners and ministers in many contemporary Christian communities. One of the potentially creative characteristics of liturgy as a form of communication is its capacity to engage all age levels. However we identify the stages of personal development (children, teenagers, young adults, the middle-aged, the elderly, etc), all of these, except perhaps the youngest of babies, is capable of contributing to liturgical communication. Moreover, teenagers today have very different talents and needs to teenagers twenty years ago. The elderly of today, similarly, live in a different cultural, medical, psychological, and political world from the elderly of twenty years ago.

Single-age Eucharists, such as Eucharists for youth or school Eucharists, can easily be highly participative. Multi-generational Eucharists are symbolically much more complex. A common and unhealthy solution often adopted in contemporary communities is that the elderly plan and run their Sunday Eucharists for what best suits them, that is, for the elderly. Other age groups, especially the young, then become the 'church of the future', that is, they don't count now but can expect to count sometime in the future.

This book sets out to examine the possibilities of active participation in Eucharist in such a way that the community maintains its interlocking connections with the wider church, including their common liturgical roots in the past, but at the same time respects and enhances the specific (often multi-cultural and usually multi-generational) identity of the local community. The bottom line though is that planners and ministers of the local community accept a responsibility to their own community that no centralized church authority can know about. This is the hands-on, week-by-week, practical liturgical action in which the local community maintains the hospitable, inclusive, and outgoing features of its Eucharists.

The ritual context

The earlier part of this chapter was intended to direct our attention at the historical facet of the context in which today we pursue the aim of active participation. The rest of this chapter will be concerned with the second facet of the context, namely the *ritual* context.[5]

---

5. A brief summary of contemporary understandings of 'ritual' can be found in Catherine Bell, 'Ritual', in *The Blackwell Companion to the Study of Religion*, edited by Robert A Segal (Oxford: Blackwell Publishing, 2006), 397–411. A basic introduction to ritual and liturgy is contained in Bernard Cooke and Gary Macy, *Christian Symbol and Ritual: An Introduction* (New York: Oxford University Press, 2005). Readers interested in the wider and more academic discussion of ritual and liturgy especially in the European context may consult Gerard Lukken, *Rituals in Abundance: Critical Reflections on the Place, Form and Identity of Christian Ritual in Our Culture* (Leuven: Peeters, 2005).

Cultures and age-groups have conventions about how people interact with one another. There are conventions, 'rules' if you like, about how we greet one another for example—handshake, kiss, embrace, bow, nod, smile, and so on. Not to follow those conventions can give offence and can indeed be a means of offering a deliberate insult. We can of course alter them a little or play creatively with them, but to do so we need to know what they are in the first place. If I am chairing a meeting but don't know what the other people's expectations of the chair's role are, or I don't pay attention to how people are seated and where they are seated, or I don't know how to engage people's responses, the results are likely to be very different from the ones I hoped for.

People come to Eucharist with a set of expectations not just of what will happen there, but also of what *ought* to happen there: what is 'proper', what is legitimate, what is acceptable, what is definitely illegitimate, what is new and wonderful. They have expectations about a range of symbolic behaviour that is creatively inventive, and a similar range that is 'mad', 'bad' or destructive. Being barefoot in church is an act of respect in some communities, but improper in others. In some communities clapping in Eucharist is acceptable; in others it is bad. In some communities bodily swaying and gesticulating is acceptable; in others it is mad. Liturgical planners operate within an awareness of these expectations or doom themselves to failure. These expectations can of course be changed—but changed successfully only by those who also know the rules (expectations) of change.

Later chapters will deal with more specific expectations of Sunday Eucharist and acceptable change. This chapter is concerned at a broader level with the main dimensions of the Eucharist ritual that we will need to attend to in order to achieve acceptable change or acceptable maintenance. We propose here to deal with four major dimensions of Eucharist that need the careful attention of the liturgical planner or minister:

   a) Eucharist as *communication*,
   b) Eucharist as *transformation*,
   c) Eucharist as *negotiation*, and
   d) Eucharist as *identity formation*.

Eucharist as communication

The liturgy of Eucharist is made up of symbolic actions—actions and words that are not primarily instrumental or technical but that convey *meaning*. They are not purely practical like using a fork or tying up one's shoes. Rather they convey information or invitation or challenge or expectation. They communicate something to and ask something of the participants. There is seldom much disagreement about this. It is part of what we have traditionally understood as a sacrament. But we should notice two trends in understanding how this works.

One trend is to see Eucharist as a 'channel of grace' in the sense that when it is done properly it creates access to God. Another trend is to see Eucharist as 'communication' in the sense that it is through responding to the meaning of those symbolic actions that we have access to God. These two views are not by any means contradictory or exclusive. But they do affect the way we go about liturgical planning and performance. If the actions of Eucharist, when performed properly, are channels of grace, then the planners and ministers need to be concerned primarily with doing it *properly*. Everything else is helpful but not really necessary.

If, on the other hand, we emphasise that Eucharist is sacramental in the sense of communicating meaning to the participants, then the planners and ministers of Eucharist need to be very concerned that these actions actually *communicate* with the participants. The first view tends to go along with sacramental minimalism (let us concentrate on the things that really count—usually what the priest does), the second tends towards sacramental maximalism (everything counts but in varying degrees).

Liturgical planners usually do pay as much attention as is practicable to all the symbols that occur in Eucharist. This means paying attention not just to major symbolic objects like the bread and wine or to the proclamation of Scripture. It means paying attention to all the symbolism of Eucharist that impacts on our senses of sight, hearing, touch, smell, taste, and kinaesthesia. The main symbolic systems that concern us relate to the use of space, furniture, object symbols (like bread, wine, Bible), movement of persons and objects, gesture, posture, speech (what is said and who speaks), music, dress, colour, odour, and noise. All of these contribute to the communication that occurs in Eucharist. We give attention to all this symbolism not just for aesthetic reason—to make it more beautiful or more attractive. We do so for the purpose of communication—we are communicating here with one another about our deepest beliefs and values. And the origin of these beliefs and values is the self-revelation of God.

Eucharist as transformation

Traditionally, sacraments have been understood as 'efficacious' in the sense that they are actions of God and of the church and therefore do not rely on the worthiness of the individual ministers. This is summed up in the traditional saying that sacraments 'signify what they effect and effect what they signify'. There is nothing automatic or magical about this. It simply means that sacraments communicate the beliefs and values of the community assembled in faith and in so doing transform the lives of that community. This is going further than saying Eucharist is communication. It is also transformation—changing people for the better.

The realists among us might want to register a hesitation here. Most of us know or at least strongly suspect that Eucharist is not always effective in our lives. Sometimes it doesn't seem to make much difference and sometimes we think we might be worse off afterwards than we were before. Traditionally it was recognised that sacraments can fail because of some basic defect and they were then said to be invalid or illicit, that is, not in fact actions of God or the church even if they appeared to be. A sacrament could also be said to be 'unfruitful', that is, I was not receptive to it at the time or not in a fit state to be affected by it. We need to concede that while Eucharist is intended to be transformative it is not always transformative in fact. But that is not to say it simply fails. Eucharist may not be effective in the sense intended, but it is nearly always a powerful ritual and will therefore have *unintended* effects.

This is a dimension of Eucharist that liturgical planners and ministers need to take very seriously. If Eucharist is not in fact transformative, not in fact changing us for the better, it may be harmful—or some parts of it may be harmful. It is seldom simply ineffective or neutral. Sexist or racist language used by a leader in Eucharist, for example, or exclusion of some people from ministry, may be neither transformative nor neutral, but offensive and demeaning to some members of the community. Here we come to the heart of the responsibility of liturgical planners and ministers. Eucharist is intended to be transformative of both individual participants and the community itself, but it may instead be harmful in some part or in some degree. And if it is indeed harmful, it would be unwise to think that this is God's fault; it is primarily a result of bad liturgical planning and/or bad performance by the ministers.

Eucharist as negotiation

'Negotiation' is not a word we normally apply to Eucharist and it may seem to imply too much a sense of the marketplace. We use it here because it calls our attention to neglected aspects of Eucharist which terms like worship, celebration, or sacrament tend to cover over. Eucharist is not like a discussion or polite debate which we leave amicably with something to think about. It includes sharing, conflict, and trade-offs of the participants' basic values and allegiances. The concept of 'negotiation' highlights the point that in Eucharist (a) we may influence one another in quite deep and disturbing ways, and (b) our basic beliefs, our lifestyles, our alliances, our purposes in life are at stake here. Our beliefs and their consequences for everyday behaviour are confirmed as valuable or put at risk during the communications which occur during regular Sunday Eucharists.

Some participants will have stronger negotiating power than others, but they have this only because the others permit it. Some participants will try to minimise or even eliminate the negotiating power of others. This is the 'I'm in charge' position. Others will think they have no negotiating power at all— 'they won't take any notice of me'. All this is part of the negotiation of power that is one of the dimensions of Eucharist. Liturgical planners need both to notice it and to be able to deal with it.

Eucharist is not the only place in which such negotiation takes place. It takes place also in the meetings, seminars, retreats, and social occasions of that same community. But in the Christian community the regular Sunday Eucharist is the place where most other negotiations receive their strongest affirmation and authorisation or are silenced. Discussions about the important roles of laity in the church, for example, are trivial if this importance is never apparent in the Sunday liturgy. Liturgical planners and ministers need to recognise when these negotiations are being initiated and where they are played out. Claims to authority, calls on official texts, cultural or generational representation, hierarchical ordering and their like are part of this negotiation. In all this, liturgical planners may need to be particularly alert to instances of the abuse of negotiating power on the one hand and cases of powerless frustration on the other.

Eucharist as identity formation

Christian identity is not simply inherited or genetically or culturally transmitted. It is developed, constructed, created, adapted and formed. At a liturgical level this occurs initially through the sacraments of Initiation. It is maintained and modified both for the individual and for the community primarily through the Sunday Eucharists. It is at Eucharist also that this identity can be most seriously distorted or destroyed. The symbolism of the Sunday Eucharist will reveal the community's basic beliefs and attitudes towards God, humanity, the Earth, and towards the community itself. Participation in Eucharist is a powerful statement of belonging to the Christian community. The Eucharist will reveal, at least partially, how this community is organised—its leadership, ministries, politics, and mission to the world. Their Eucharists will also display the foundations of their identity—their foundational books (the Scriptures, other church documents) and their historic origins (in the life of Jesus of Nazareth)—and how they interpret these foundations for contemporary living.

Everything liturgical planners and ministers do with the symbolic actions of Eucharist will add to or detract from this sense of identity or sense of belonging of this community including its sense of identification with other local communities, the local diocese, and the universal church.

Conclusion

This chapter has been concerned with the context, the ground rules, within which we seek to achieve active participation in Eucharist. It has called attention to the particular historical crossroads at which contemporary liturgy now stands: a restoration of former styles of liturgy or a continuing renewal enriched by cultural diversity both contemporary and traditional. The chapter has also founded liturgical planning in a ritual context where Eucharist can be seen as an interaction of which the important dimensions are communication, transformation, negotiation and identity formation.

Key questions:

1) In what sense are we at an historical crossroads in how we celebrate Eucharist? Are the two currents of restoration and renewal apparent in our own celebrations of Eucharist?
2) What are we paying particular attention to in each case when we regard Eucharist as (a) communication, (b) transformation, (c) negotiation, and (d) identity formation?
3) What are the most powerful ways in which our own celebration of Eucharist enhances each of these four dimensions of Eucharist

Chapter 3
The Christian Assembly and its Ministries

This chapter is concerned with the nature of the assembly, that is, the gathering of people who come together for Eucharist, and the various ways they take part in it. It focuses particularly on the kinds of ministry that operate within the assembly and on the qualifications and formation for ministry. A more detailed examination of particular ministries is left to later chapters on The Rites of Gathering and Sending (Chapter 4), The Liturgy of the Word (Chapter 5) and The Liturgy of Eucharist (Chapter 6).

The assembly celebrates the Eucharist

The term 'assembly' refers to the people who gather together face-to-face at a particular time and place for liturgy. Many of the people who make up that assembly already live in social relationships which began before that assembly, will persist after it, and continue outside of it. This wider, more continuous group of people we refer to as the local 'community'. An assembly then is a gathering of members of a Christian community in a particular place and time for a liturgy.

It is primarily the assembly, rather than any one particular person or role or ministry or church leader, which celebrates Eucharist. Liturgical planners in the past have often worked out of an assumption that it is the ordained priest who is the primary celebrant of the liturgy so that the priest is above the assembly rather than part of it. This book is based on the principle that the liturgy belongs primarily to the assembly. The assembly contains *within* it the priest, various ministers, and congregation. Behind this principle is the understanding that the liturgical assembly is constituted by the Holy Spirit when the baptised gather in the name of Jesus Christ in thanksgiving to their Creator. We need then to give more attention than we have in the past to who makes up the liturgical assembly and the various roles within it.[1]

Ways of participating

The assembly that celebrates Eucharist is not simply a mass of people acting in unison. Nor, on the other hand, is it a collection of individuals acting at random. It has its own internal structure of varying roles and common expectations. This structure includes different degrees of participation. Participation is not about everybody being the same, nor even about everybody being equal. There are options here for people about the way they participate in Eucharist and the *degree* to which they participate. Here too are decisions for liturgy planners and community leaders about how this structure actually works best in their own particular circumstances.

There are some basic degrees of participation that will be present in most Sunday Eucharists. Liturgical planners will normally need to take note of at least five kinds of participants in a liturgical assembly. We may refer to these as

- observers
- general participants
- recipients
- ministers, and
- leaders.

Each of these terms refers to a different *kind* of participation in a liturgical assembly. Each also implies a different degree of participation. Observers are the least intensely involved, while recipients, ministers, and leaders are the most intensely involved either in the sense that they have a greater degree of responsibility for the liturgical action or in the sense that they are a particular focus of attention.

---

1. Contemporary understanding of the assembly with its origins in ancient theology and church documents is discussed in Judith M Kubicki, *The Presence of Christ in the Gathered Assembly* (New York/London: Continuum, 2006). Another recent source for the history of the idea of the liturgical assembly and the way it is dealt with in official church documents is Catherine Vincie, *Celebrating Divine Mystery: A Primer in Liturgical Theology* (Collegeville, Minnesota: Liturgical Press, 2009), 19–50.

Observers are those people who are physically present in the assembly but are psychologically maintaining some distance from it. Sometimes people are there because of an obligation to some other person—teenagers who wish they didn't have to be there, non-members who are there mainly to support their spouses, people there for some social or political advantage, people on their way out of the church who haven't quite taken the final step, or 'seekers' who are making up their minds whether they wish to belong or not. This is the least committed degree of participation. It is still different though from not being there are all. Their presence there is still signalled by a number of ritual signs or the absence of them—not taking part in common gestures and postures, not knowing common responses, disengaged facial expression, and so on. Psychologically and socially these observers are at the edge of the liturgical action. They may literally occupy the outer edges or be near the doors of the liturgical space. Though observers are at the edge of the assembly they are not irrelevant to it since they often affect the attention, attitudes and behaviour of the participants—perhaps as a depressing indifference, as uplifting witness of fidelity to another person, or as interested but uncommitted bystander. When there are a large number of observers at a liturgy it may radically affect its atmosphere as is notoriously the case, for example, at a wedding or funeral when there are many people with no church connections.

We use the term *general participants* to refer to those people who are actively engaged in the liturgical action but do not take on any particular role or ministry within it. These people identify with the liturgical action as their own, they are personally engaged in it rather than merely observers of it. Their engagement in the liturgy occurs through actions in common such as movement together, singing together, praying common prayers, sitting and standing together. Usually these general participants will be the largest category of people taking part in Eucharist and as such have a major impact on how it works. It is largely their attention to and engagement in the liturgy that constitutes the 'atmosphere' of the liturgy. This atmosphere will also be full of gracious and prayerful energy depending on these participants. It is their active participation in the Eucharist and their capacity to be receptive to that liturgy that is the main objective of liturgical planners and ministers. The way they regard one another, the way they pray together or sing together is a main component of successful liturgy. This is made up of a myriad of liturgical signs, most of which are not spelt out in liturgical books and many of which are beyond the control of the liturgical leaders.

The term *recipients* refers here to those people to whom the liturgical action is directed in some specific and explicit way. In Eucharist the 'communicants' are such specific recipients of the liturgical action. In other major Christian liturgies such as Baptism, Anointing of the Sick, Marriage, Funerals, or Ordination these recipients are more clearly singled out than in Eucharist. Still, during a Eucharist, as well as communicants there may also be other kinds of recipients such as people commissioned for ministries or for mission, people baptised, and people who are the focus of attention because of some particular event such as a jubilee or anniversary.

Ministers

The rest of this chapter is dedicated mainly to the roles of liturgical *ministers* in the Eucharist. One of the strongest features of recent liturgical reform has been the revitalising of ministries, both in the variety of ministries that are now regularly part of Eucharist and in the number of people engaged in any particular ministry. But one of the points of practical contention today has become whether these new ministries are treated as ministries in their own right or simply regarded as subordinate to the priest-presider.

Ministers are those people who, in addition to the communal actions of general participants, also fulfill some particular role within the assembly. These are the people who perform special roles in that they actively do something *for* or *to* or *on behalf* of the other participants. In a Sunday Eucharist there will usually be several such roles which are distinguished from the common participation in the liturgy. These may be, for example, the preacher, the Scripture readers, the communion ministers, the collectors, the bearers of gifts, the choir leader, the cantor, the musicians, the ushers, and those who say various prayers on behalf of others. Some of these ministries are quite brief in duration and involve some very specific liturgical action. Others will be of longer duration and require more complex liturgical and leadership skills.

Liturgical leader is a term for those particular kinds of ministry that include an overall responsibility for the whole or a major part of the liturgy. They usually include an oversight or coordination of other ministries. Traditionally this has been the role of the 'priest', or in more contemporary terms, the 'presider'. We will look more specifically at the role of leader in Chapter Seven.

Qualifications for ministry

Liturgical planners are commonly faced with the question, Who should be liturgical ministers? And sometimes the more agonizing question, Who should not? There are often volunteers who should not be ministers. And there are people who would make good ministers but won't ever volunteer. Every local community will have some process of discernment, however simple it might be, for who should and who should not be liturgical ministers. A key element in this process is clarity about the qualifications for ministry. A set of qualifications is often something of an ideal. But it is not an ideal in the sense of a fantasyland. It is an ideal in the sense of a goal that the community will set out to achieve over a number of years. What then are the qualifications for being a liturgical minister?

The approach we suggest here in answer to this question is a 'skills-based' approach. In effect this means that the central qualification for liturgical ministers is competence at doing the job. Competence needs to be supported and tempered however by two other qualifications: *representation* and *witness*.

This might look obvious. Who wants incompetent ministers? Yet in practice the priorities are sometimes reversed. The worst kind of process is when people become ministers simply because they volunteered for it. The opposite extreme is when the priest or a community leader simply taps the shoulder of anyone they think might be prepared to accept it. More common probably is where people are chosen because they are good, faithful members of the community. This is effectively giving priority to the qualification of 'witness'. Another common process is where people are asked to be ministers because more people from a particular ethnic group or more youth or more men or more women are needed. Effectively this is to give priority to the qualification of 'representation'.

People who perform a liturgical ministry can either enhance or harm the spiritual life of the community. The primary reason for choosing a person for a ministry, we suggest, is usually *competence*, that is, that they are better than anyone else in that community at performing this service *well*. Readers, for example, are competent if a) they are themselves dedicated students of Scripture, and b) they read publicly in such a way that the rest of the assembly understands the reading better than they could possibly do by reading it themselves.

Most ministries require what we might call both a 'practical' competence and a 'personal' competence. *Practical* competence is simply the skill to perform well in a liturgical setting. A church usher or a person who greets people at the entrance of the church needs the public relations skills of welcoming and guiding people amidst a gathering of many people. A reader needs the skill of communicating the meaning of a reading to a gathered group of listeners—a very different skill from reading the Bible at home or reading in a small home group. *Personal* competence is the educational or community background that lies behind and precedes the public performance. To continue with the example of readers, the personal competence required in this case is the reader's personal familiarity with and ability to interpret the Scriptures before they come to the point of reading liturgically.

This focus on competence needs to be supported and tempered by the qualifications of 'witness' and 'representation'. Competence on its own, in other words, is not enough.

The qualification of *witness* means that the minister's life outside the community is congruent with the beliefs and values of that community. There needs to be congruence, a 'fit', between what people do in liturgy and the way they lead the rest of their lives. Any liturgical minister is part of the 'face' that the community presents to itself and to society at large. A liturgical minister whose lifestyle is publicly at odds with a Christian way of life is a counter-witness to that community. Put more positively, a liturgical minister whose lifestyle is a good witness to Christianity brings a quality to their liturgical ministry that enhances their service to the community. A communion minister whose lifestyle is compassionate, for example, brings a quality and immediate authenticity to their ministry that sheer competence does not achieve.

The qualification of *representation* refers to the way in which the ministers as a whole reflect back to the community its own diverse make-up of members. Put negatively, if all liturgical ministers belong to the same ethnic group when the community itself is multi-ethnic, this displays an ethnically prejudiced community. A similar judgment can be made in terms of age-groups or gender. The process by which a community works towards fulfilling its need for ministers will include redressing the imbalances in representation that occur from time to time such as changes in the ethnic composition of the community, unintended shifts towards gender imbalance, changes in age-groups and the community's perception of age-group responsibilities.

The balances between these three qualifications of competence, witness, and representation are slightly different for each particular ministry. The ministry of reader, for example, has a high need for competence in Scripture interpretation and public reading skills. The other qualifications of witness and representation do not usually compensate for reading that can't be understood. This is usually true also of musicians and choir or singing group leaders. High competence is required here and can seldom be compensated for by witness and only in special cases by representation. Communion ministry, on the other hand, does not require such a high level of competence in acquired skills. There are numerous people who already have the behavioural skills of respectful and gracious interaction needed for that ministry. But it does require high levels of both witness of life and representation of diversity since these are so intimately related to the nature of communion in the Body of Christ.

Preparation and formation of ministers

Two of the major dimensions of liturgy noted in the previous chapter are that it is about communication and transformation. If a liturgy can communicate well, it can also communicate badly. While it is intended to be transformative, badly done liturgy may also be bad for us. When we say 'badly' here this does not mean just aesthetically bad in the sense that it is ugly or banal or uninteresting. It may also be bad in the sense that it has a harmful rather than a beneficial effect on us.

If a particular celebration of Eucharist is harmful rather than transformative, this will be due in large part to the actions of the ministers. One of the practices in the past has been that prospective ministers were expected to take part in preparation, usually of a practical kind, before they began their ministry, but after that were left largely to their own devices. The reason for this was usually that people are busy and it's hard to find time for ministry formation. In effect, this is a belief that ministries aren't that important anyway and therefore neither is ministry formation.

While admitting that there are practical difficulties, we suggest that the results of bad liturgical ministry are too costly to the community at large to be acceptable. Ministry formation is necessary and it has four main stages:

a) preparation before people are commissioned for ministry;
b) ongoing in-service formation so that understanding and skills are continually being enhanced and initial inadequacies redressed;
c) regular discussions and decisions by the ministers themselves about improvements to liturgical performance;
d) a regular liturgical commissioning of ministers within a Sunday Eucharist where the ministers publicly commit themselves to the ministry for a set period of time.

Some kind of *preparation* is the least controversial element in this list of educational requirements and nearly all local communities will have some way of doing this at least for the higher profile ministries. Some of the ministries like collectors or those who present the gifts at the Liturgy of Eucharist may not need much preparation. Once these have become an established practice and people see them in operation every Sunday they may be better learnt simply by observation. And they do provide ministerial involvement for those who are unable or disinclined for whatever reason to take part in courses and training sessions.

The need for *ongoing education* is more often overlooked or put into the 'too hard' basket. For most liturgical ministries a commitment to ongoing formation is necessary both on the part of the community leaders and on the part of the ministers themselves. Except in the case where ministers are salaried employees, it is practical and legitimate that most of the ministerial education will be in-service and ongoing rather than a pre-requisite, long-term preparation. A reliance on in-service training means some lack of competence while new ministers learn the role. It has the advantage though of providing an ongoing process of education that can cope with change and in which many people can play the role of mentor for new ministers.

Regular discussion and decisions by the ministers themselves about improvements to liturgical performance, is one of the main ways of enhancing the transformative value of the Sunday Eucharist. After some experience, the ministers themselves become the primary liturgical educators. Teachers of liturgy and theology still play an informative role, but they may lack the hands-on knowledge of symbolic communication that the ministers themselves rapidly acquire.

A regular liturgical commissioning of ministers within a Sunday Eucharist has two complementary effects. Firstly, it provides that ministers publicly commit themselves to faithfully perform their ministry for a specified period of time. It would be odd in any case if liturgical ministers were not appointed liturgically. This would imply that the community leaders concerned with liturgy were ignoring the transformative power of liturgy in appointing liturgical ministers. Secondly, it makes public before the whole local community who their ministers are and what they are committed to perform. These commissionings are best done with a known regularity and we suggest that this be annually or at most every two years.

Recruitment and retirement

Recruitment to and retirement from liturgical ministry are among the most psychologically and socially difficult questions for liturgical planners. The key ingredient in a policy of recruitment of liturgical ministers is clarity about the qualifications for ministry and a long-term approach to achieving the ideal. We have proposed above that these qualifications be competence, witness, and representation. Those responsible for recruitment however always need to allow flexibility rather than apply rigid standards. Looking for a balance among competence, witness, and representation helps to do this.

The issue of retirement from ministry has two faces. Existing ministers need a normal, rather than traumatic, way in which they can exit a ministry without facing contrary exhortations or recriminations. Some communities assume their ministers will carry on forever. Others have a non-renewal term (such as two years) so that people can't go on forever. Neither of these is satisfactory. An annual commissioning liturgy that includes a commitment to a one or two-year term, allows ministers to renew their commitment for a further period, or retire from ministry by simply not renewing. It also allows a retired minister to return at a later date as their life circumstances change.

The other face of the issue of retirement is the one that confronts community leaders with oversight of the community ministries. From this point of view there is need for a compassionate way in which an unsuitable person can be retired from ministry or transferred to a more suitable ministry with the least possible personal hurt. Unsuitable ministers cannot simply be left in ministry to the detriment of the community, but dismissals can be abusive and there is need for an accountable procedure for involuntary retirement from ministry. An annual commissioning along with the discussions and interactions that precede it as the list of ministers is compiled and confirmed can be part of this procedure. It at least allows both renewal and retirement to be regarded as normal with minimal recrimination, embarrassment, or personal hurt.

Conclusion

The Christian assembly that celebrates Eucharist is structured by varying degrees and ways of participation. While everyone contributes to the active participation that creates that assembly, the part played by ministers is particularly important and needs special attention from liturgical planners. While skilful service, or competence, is of major importance in most ministries, the fact that the variety of ministers represents the variety of the community enhances the hospitable and inclusive features of the Eucharist. The ministers' witness of life enhances in particular the outgoing or missionary feature of Eucharist.

In terms of the historical context of current liturgical planning, the stance taken in this chapter is towards continuing renewal of liturgy in the direction of greater participation and diversity rather than a restoration of a single presider model of Eucharist. In terms of the ritual context, this chapter has emphasised the need for clarity and transparency in ministry recruitment, formation and retirement so that Eucharist may be indeed transformative and continually contribute to the formation of the Christian identity of that community.

Key questions:
1) What are the different ways or degrees of participation in the assembly? How do they occur in our own assembly?
2) What qualifications are needed for ministry and how are they balanced for each of the main ministries in Eucharist? What is the policy or practice of our own community?
3) The preparation and formation of ministers is a process involving what main stages? What is the process for our own community?
4) How can we best handle the recruitment and retirement of ministers?

Chapter 4
The Rites of Gathering and Sending

In this chapter we take a closer look at the beginning and ending phases of Eucharist. Rather than simply 'Introductory Rites' we refer to the beginning phase of Eucharist in which the assembly is gathered together as the 'Rite of Gathering'. We refer to the concluding phase of Eucharist as the 'Rite of Sending' since it is here that the assembly is sent back out on its mission to the world from which it was gathered.

The whole Eucharist celebration thus moves through a sequence of four main phases:

- The Rite of Gathering opens the celebration and continues up to the Collect Prayer.
- The Liturgy of the Word begins with the Scripture readings and continues through to the Prayer of the Faithful.
- The Liturgy of Eucharist begins at the preparation of the gifts and continues through to the end of the Communion Rite.
- The Rite of Sending begins after Communion and concludes the formal liturgy.

Gathering the assembly

The Gathering Rite is shorter than the Liturgy of the Word and the Liturgy of Eucharist that follow and is often treated as of lesser importance. In a sense this is true, but it has its own indispensable contribution to the Eucharist as a whole. When we hear stories of people who immediately felt excluded by the words or musical style of the entrance hymn or make statements such as, 'I went there to Mass and no one spoke to me' or 'I felt I was in a foreign country' or who conversely say 'I felt totally at ease from the time they handed me the leaflet at the door' or 'I immediately felt welcome' we begin to sense how much the Gathering Rite is the gateway into effective participation in the Liturgies of Word and Eucharist.

The standard introductory rites of the Eucharist consist of some combination of

- the Entrance
- Greetings
- the Act of Penitence
- the 'Kyrie' litany
- the 'Gloria' hymn of praise
- the Collect Prayer.

In line with this standard structure we sometimes think of the Eucharist as beginning with the entrance song or the greeting of the liturgical leader. But this is only the formal beginning of the liturgy. The real rites of gathering begin earlier and more informally when people acknowledge and greet one another on the road or in the car park as they move towards the church. The sense in which the Eucharist is hospitable or otherwise begins there before any formal opening by a liturgical minister.

The greeting at the door, the ease with which people can be seated, the sense of belonging they experience, the atmosphere of readiness or anticipation all send to the gathering people powerful messages about their place and their participation in this event. The hospitality of Eucharist is offered by the people to one another and creates the atmosphere of the gathering. It is in these initial greetings that the assembly begins to exercise its role as the 'celebrant' of the liturgy—as its members take responsibility for the quality of the liturgy by offering an inclusive hospitality to one another.

In these initial encounters people already begin to communicate the identity of this community. The style of these encounters depends on existing local traditions such as cultural and age-group traditions of how people are used to greeting one another anyway in everyday life: with reserve, with enthusiasm, immediately friendly or with formal respect, with a handshake, a bow, an embrace, a kiss. Here too a variety of cultures may already begin to encounter one another.

Another set of traditions derives from the architecture of the church. This will already have created expectations such as whether this is a place of community interaction or whether it is a place of prayerful silence. The way the pews or chairs are arranged inside the church and the positioning of the tabernacle also affect expectations of how people gather. Often these are inherited from an earlier community who had different views on the proper use of space and furniture and the ways people interrelate within them.

Contemporary liturgical planners need to work respectfully with existing cultural, age-related, and architectural traditions, but their decisions can still greatly improve active participation in Eucharist at this early stage. One decision, for example, is whether to leave these initial encounters to the free flow of people or to organise ministers such as ushers and 'greeters' who welcome people at the door. Such ministers usually increase active participation in Eucharist and a sense of welcome, but they can also be intrusive and over-formalise a community that is already skilled at informal greeting. Where there are such ministers, their personal and social skills make a significant contribution to the sense of hospitality and inclusiveness that characterises, or is lacking in, the community's Eucharists.

Pattern and challenge: the formal structure of gathering

The entrance of the liturgical ministers, or an entrance hymn, or an opening greeting by a liturgical minister signal the shift from the relative informality of people entering the church to a more formal liturgical mode. The standard introductory rites listed above present liturgical ministers with both a structure and a challenge. This standard structure establishes a pattern of familiarity in which most of the people can feel at home.

It also presents a challenge to liturgical ministers. In a very short space of time and relatively few words these initial rites establish a sense of the identity of this assembly. And here lies the challenge. The opening words can indicate a sense of ecclesiastical formality or boring repetition, a declaration that nothing interesting is ever likely to happen here. They may lock the assembly into a tired passivity from which that celebration of Eucharist will never recover. Or they may establish a sense that something important is about to happen, something that engages our lives, something that we belong to and that belongs to us. The challenge for liturgical planners and ministers is to create a Gathering Rite that has a sense of the familiar in its formal structure, but also claims the engagement of the congregation. It can claim this engagement if it is a rite of welcome and orientation.[1]

---

1. Readers unfamiliar with local adaptations of the Gathering Rite will find a description of the Zairean adaptations in Leon Ngoy Kalumba, 'The Zairean Rite: The Roman Missal for the Dioceses of Zaire (Congo)', in *Liturgy in a Postmodern World*, edited by Keith Pecklers (London/New York: Continuum, 2003), 92–98.

Welcome and orientation

The sense of *welcome* has already begun before the formal part of the liturgy begins. It is reinforced, or contradicted, by all the signals of inclusion and exclusion that occur during the more formal part of the Gathering Rite. Is this assembly gender-inclusive, culture-inclusive, and age-inclusive? What kind of community is this that has gathered here? Is this a community that believes in the equality and complementarity of women and men? The use of gender-inclusive language and the inclusion of both men and women in the ministries of the Gathering Rite will affirm or deny this. Is this a community that believes primarily in an almighty Father God, or does it have more inclusive images of God? The opening Sign of the Cross and the words of the 'Gloria' or hymn of praise will demonstrate this. The Father-Lord-King image of God portrayed in the standard Sign of the Cross and Gloria present a narrow-focused, exclusive image of God from which the rest of the liturgy may never recover. Most liturgical planners will want to change this language to more inclusive and expansive images of God in their Gathering Rite.[2]

Other language issues can also be settled here. Are there other language groups besides English that should be acknowledged? How formal or engaging is the language of greetings and prayers? Many of the official Collect Prayers, for example, which bring the Gathering Rite to a conclusion, are dull and repetitious, and often they are prayed in a correspondingly disinterested way. If liturgical planners and ministers are content with this, they are signalling to the whole congregation that our relationship with God is similarly dull, requiring dutiful repetition rather than creative engagement. How dull is this God who welcomes us here? It is worth recalling here occasions when we have heard the power of the English language spoken as real contemporary poetry—spoken simply yet creatively, engagingly, artistically, memorably. Why not here then in these Collect Prayers? What kind of God might we then expect in response?[3]

---

2. Proposals for how we might go about developing a more adequate range of language and images of God are suggested in Catherine Vincie, *Celebrating Divine Mystery: A Primer in Liturgical Theology* (Collegeville, Minnesota: Liturgical Press, 2009), 81–100.
3. The issue of literal English translations from the Latin and a critique of the principles espoused in the Roman document *Liturgiam Authenticam* is addressed in Nathan D Mitchell, 'The Amen Corner: "But Is It English?"', in *Worship* 81/1 (2007): 69–83.

The Gathering Rite also sets the *orientation* of this particular Eucharist in the sense that it incorporates the life of this particular community into the Eucharist liturgy of the universal church. This is not usually the place for 'The theme of the Mass this morning is . . .'. That is a matter for the Liturgy of the Word. This phase of Eucharist is mainly about the assembly itself rather than the Scripture Readings. Are there special events, special seasons, or special people to be acknowledged in this assembly? Is there some special addition to this Sunday Eucharist that is not usually there and warrants more than simply an inclusion in the Prayer of the Faithful?—an anniversary, a baptism, a commissioning of ministers? Is there something special to be remembered in this Eucharist? Is this a special celebration for some section of the community, a thanksgiving for some event in the community, the liturgical season, the season of the Earth's cycle?

This is also where the signals are first given for the style of Eucharist that people can expect here. Is it to be formal, stiff, reserved, friendly, prayerful, exciting, agitated, unsure of its own identity? Most important here is the orientation to God that is established at the beginning of the Eucharist. Do we emphasise a penitential relationship, or a relationship of praise and thanksgiving, or some combination of these? What are the images of God that are presented here? These are not matters of simply following the official formulas, but of establishing the orientation of this assembly on this particular Sunday.

When the liturgical ministers are able to blend the life and style of this particular community's events with the formal structure of the Roman Rite they engage the community in active attention and participation. Even more importantly and at a more fundamental level, they demonstrate a due respect for this local community and the Spirit of God that enlivens it.

Ultimately, the ministers of this Gathering Rite are aiming to gather a community in the presence of God, a community with a strong and deep sense of who their God is and who they are. There seem to be many possibilities and many ways of doing this. But in any case it should not be cluttered. It is the quality of words and actions that count, not the quantity. It does not take more words to be careful about how we address God than it does to repeat the formalities. Nor is it a matter of getting everything done every Sunday. The ministers of this Rite will need to leave some things out and include other things according to the liturgical seasons and the rhythm of life of this community.

The ministers of the Gathering Rite

Probably the most important decision liturgical planners will make about the Gathering Rite is to do with the *ministers* of this rite. A successful welcome and orientation as described above requires considerable skill and knowledge of the community. It is unlikely that it can be achieved by any one person. Few would dispute that the musicians play a vital part in establishing the spirit of the assembly in its Gathering Rite. It is often assumed though that the only other minister involved will be the priest presider. But should this be so? A Gathering Rite in which the person who welcomes people, leads the Act of Penitence and prays the Collect Prayer is always a male priest from one ethnic group is an exclusive liturgy. The Gathering Rite needs a variety of skilled ministers and the ordained priest need not always be its leader.

The regular Sunday Eucharist becomes hospitable to all people when the people who play the role of host, the people who lead this Gathering Rite, include women and men, members of the major ethnic groups that make up the community, and a variety of personality types who bring their own variety to that welcome and orientation—not every Sunday of course, but from time to time. The experience of being greeted and welcomed into worship by someone like ourselves heightens awareness of the co-responsibility of the whole assembly for the celebration of the liturgy.

None of this is accomplished of course in a single Sunday Eucharist. Over months and years of regular Sunday Eucharists this sense of hospitable welcome and of identity is built up in a variety of ways. It is the variety of ways of addressing God, the acknowledgment of cultures that takes place at different times, the variety of music styles that suit different age groups, and respect for the spiritual quality of this community that add up to a welcoming community sure of its own identity and comfortable with its own diversity.

Sending the assembly out: the Rite of Sending

The Rite of Sending, like the Rite of Gathering, is relatively short in its official form and often not given much attention in liturgical planning. After the Liturgies of the Word and Eucharist that precede it, it may seem that what is needed here is just a quick fade-out. Indeed the standard concluding rites of the Eucharist consisting of the announcements then a blessing and words of dismissal indicate a rather functional conclusion without much fuss. Yet the Sending Rite can serve to focus the whole purpose of Eucharist in its outreach towards the wider world. The purpose of this assembly lies beyond here in the mission of the Christian community to the world.

Liturgical planners face a small but telling decision here on the structure of this Sending Rite. In the Roman Missal, the *Prayer after Communion* is treated as the conclusion to the Communion Rite. It appears then as a formal way for the presider to bring the Communion Rite to an end. This is often indicated in the content of these Prayers many of which pray that we be in some way changed for the better as a result of this Communion—that, for example, this Eucharist may help our eternal redemption, that it may keep us faithful, or that the sacrament we have received may bring us health of mind and body. Many of these are, in other words, prayers for ourselves.

Sometimes however these official Prayers pray not so directly for ourselves but rather for our mission in the world as a result of this Eucharist—that, for example, this Eucharist give the faith continued growth throughout the world, or help us to bring God's salvation and joy to all the world.[4] It greatly strengthens the Sending Rite if this Prayer is treated not as a conclusion to the Communion Rite on its own, but rather as part of the Sending Rite, that is, a conclusion to the Eucharist as a whole. The content of this Prayer would then become a prayer for the community's outreach to the world. It could indicate the direction of that outreach, not just in a general way, but more specifically as an outward focus for the particular themes that have already appeared in this particular celebration of Eucharist.

Where liturgical planners do regard the Prayer after Communion as part of the Sending Rite, they may need to edit and sometimes alter considerably the wording of this sending Prayer so that it is focused on the mission to the wider world. When this happens the content of the Prayer can be connected back with the earlier Scripture Readings and homily of that particular Sunday. Combined with a final blessing that also has a strong sense of sending people out, it can then become a powerful statement of the community's mission.

The *announcements* or *notices* also point to important ingredients in the mission of a local Christian community. Some of these announcements highlight activities of the Christian community itself. Others cover activities and issues beyond the Christian community that members of the community may support. Whether it is a notice that a food bank requires certain items, or an invitation to be part of an interfaith meeting, or a prison visitors group,

---

4. An analysis of the missionary dimension of some of the official Prayers after Communion, without however any suggestion that local communities might make any changes to them, is given in James Michael Donohue, "'Help Us to Bring Your Love to the World': Exhortation to Mission in the Prayer after Communion', in *Liturgical Ministry* 18, Fall (2009): 182–90.

or information about action for justice, each of these messages extends, challenges, and reminds the assembly that as community we are about mission.

This is not meant to be a tedious time of numerous long announcements. In order to avoid this, many communities have newsletters or other means of communicating announcements. But nor should this time be treated as trivial by liturgical planners, or a time that should be reduced as much as possible, even eliminated altogether. The announcements can be an influential shaper of the identity of the community. The content and manner of these notices can declare very clearly the community's missionary identity. The announcements made here are ideally those that most pointedly and most importantly identify the mission of the community at this time.

The words of the final *blessing and dismissal* need not be simply the same formulas each Sunday. The words of the blessing can recapture the insights of the earlier parts of the liturgy or give a shortened version of the theme that has emerged throughout the liturgies of the Word and of Eucharist. The words prepared beforehand may need final alteration to capture those earlier images and messages. The assembly is thus sent out to its task, mission-focused, resolved again to take part in establishing the reign of God in the world. The liturgy changes us if we participate in it. The blessing and dismissal should indicate where that change might lie. The last words the assembly hears are then a spirited re-focusing of what has been heard and preached and prayed by the community. These function as a commission to action and to mission.

Beyond the liturgy

People who are ministers and leaders in the Gathering and Sending Rites of Eucharist act as the hosts of the assembly, the promoters and guardians of the community's identity and outreach. Once their formal liturgical role is completed their ministry enters a new phase. Liturgical ministers remain an image of the presence of God in community and continue their contribution to the community beyond the time of liturgy. The talking and networking and catching up that happen before and after Eucharist are important to their role as liturgical ministers and as those concerned for the pastoral wellbeing of the community. They do not suddenly appear at liturgy then just as suddenly disappear. Participation in the life of the community outside of the liturgy is a part of all liturgical ministry especially those ministries concerned with the gathering in and sending out of the community.

Conclusion

In the Gathering Rite the Spirit begins work among the people producing a response at once individual and shared. We suggest that the Gathering Rite is a rite of welcome and orientation. It assists the assembly to recognise their unity and their diversity in the God who calls them together. They begin then to come alive with that presence of Christ that becomes a reality when Christians gather together to pray. In their own gathering bodies they form the Body of Christ. As those gathered become aware of being unified by a common focus and a commitment to a common task, the presence of Christ deepens. But that liturgical unity is not intended to last. This is an assembly that moves forward and outwards to a mission in the wider world. The purpose of this community's mission outreach is focused and strengthened, or may be dissipated and dampened, in the Sending Rite that brings the liturgy to a close.

Key questions:

1) What is the Gathering Rite intended for and in what ways is it likely to succeed or fail? What does our community do well in this Rite and what changes could we make?
2) Should we be content with the final phase of Eucharist as simply a conclusion or is it better regarded as the final way of focusing the participants on their outreach to the wider world?
3) What are the ways in which the Gathering and Sending Rites contribute to the identity of the local community and the direction of its mission? And conversely, in what ways can they dissipate this identity and this mission? How could our own local practice be adapted?

Chapter 5
The Liturgy of the Word

By the end of the Gathering Rite we could hope that the people have become an assembly that is physically, psychologically, socially and spiritually present to one another, conscious of the divine presence in which they have gathered. The assembly can then shift its attention to the reading and interpretation of Scripture—the Liturgy of the Word. The Liturgy of the Word begins with the first Scripture Reading and concludes with the Prayer of the Faithful.

The standard rites of the Liturgy of the Word consist of:
- First Reading (commonly from the Old Testament)
- Responsorial Psalm
- Second Reading (from the New Testament)
- Acclamation before the Gospel
- Gospel Reading
- Homily
- Profession of Faith
- Prayer of the Faithful

The lectionary

An early decision for liturgical planners is which translation of the Bible will be used in the Liturgy of the Word. This is a decision about the accuracy of the translation, the accessibility of the English, and gender-inclusive language. In the case of a Liturgy of the Word specifically for children, there is also a decision about the use of a children's lectionary or Bible accessible to children. Local bishop's conferences will usually have made decisions about the accuracy and accessibility of translation suitable for liturgical reading and these can be a guide for local liturgical planners.

The issue of gender-inclusive language however often remains unresolved. Most of the older translations of the Bible contain sexist language that no longer represents an accurate translation into contemporary English. Liturgical planners will need to avoid lectionaries that contain such translations even if they are otherwise accurate and accessible. The object of this concern for the lectionary is that the liturgy be inclusive, in other words that people's listening and understanding of the Scripture Readings not be inhibited by such factors as inaccurate translation or inaccessible or sexist language.

We assume here that most communities will use the Scripture selections in the official lectionary of the Roman Rite (*Ordo Lectionum Missae*, 1969). Some liturgical planners may prefer the more recent and ecumenical *Revised Common Lectionary (1992)*.[1] An *Inclusive Readings* lectionary seeks to address discriminatory practices which contribute to racism, sexism and classicism.[2] Using a modern translation of the Bible itself without the lectionary format is also an option that allows more extended passages than are contained in the lectionary selections. We do not consider here the arguments for or against these options, but alert liturgical planners to these possibilities.[3]

A procession with the lectionary?

The Liturgy of the Word is primarily an oral proclamation of Scripture to which the assembly listens and responds. Should the lectionary itself, as 'container' of the Scriptures, also be displayed liturgically as a visual symbol? In some liturgies the lectionary itself is never seen by the congregation because it is hidden by the lectern (or 'ambo'). Provided the oral proclamation of the readings remains primary, a visual display of the lectionary can enhance people's active participation in the liturgy. Here the Liturgy of the Word can be seen in parallel with the Liturgy of the Eucharist where, provided the con-

---

1. Consultation on Common Texts, *The Revised Common Lectionary* (Nashville: Abingdon Press, 1992). For more information see the website of the Consultation on Common Texts at http://commontexts.org.
2. 'Inclusive Language Project', PO Box 1400, Toombul, QLD 4012, Australia.
3. For more background on scriptural texts in liturgy the reader may consult David N Power, '*The Word of the Lord*': *Liturgy's Use of Scripture* (Maryknoll, New York: Orbis Books, 2001).

sumption of the consecrated bread and wine is primary, a visual display of the bread and wine can also enhance people's participation.

Such a visual display of the lectionary is usually done in the form of a procession to the lectern. The issue for liturgical planners is when this should occur. In the Roman Rite there is a tradition of a procession of the book of the gospels before the Gospel Reading. Contemporary Eucharists often include a procession of the lectionary (containing all the Readings not just the Gospels) either included in the entrance procession of ministers in the Gathering Rite, or at the beginning of the Liturgy of the Word.

The most symbolically engaging of these three practices, we suggest, is a procession of the lectionary that marks the beginning of the Liturgy of the Word. This serves to turn the focus from the Gathering Rite to the Scripture Readings. It is more suitable for large assemblies than for small, intimate ones. This procession however needs to be conducted with style and confidence—something important is about to happen here! And a visual display of the lectionary needs to be followed by a similarly strong, convincing, oral presentation of its contents.

The Scripture Readings

The primary task of the readers is to ensure that the Readings are heard and understood. There is a substantial difference between someone who simply reads the words clearly, and someone who reads them with understanding and conviction. Sometimes the Scripture Readings are treated as if they are mere preliminaries to the homily. Sometimes it is not clear whether the reader actually believes in what is being read. But each of the Readings is a proclamation in its own right with messages for the listeners that will not all be picked up in the homily. Their presentation needs the care and attention to wording that comes from a reader convinced of the importance of this Reading for these people at this time—an act of public reading that is important in its own right regardless of what else may come before or after.

Even with careful, meaningful reading, the Scripture Readings still remain difficult for many people in contemporary congregations. Some of the Readings have immediate impact; but more often the language, images and stories, the customs and attitudes that lie behind them are strange to contemporary listeners. This difficulty is compounded because of the lectionary format where three relatively short passages from different parts of the Bible are presented to the congregation with only brief breaks between them. The listeners have to shift their mental focus quite quickly from one historical period to another, and from one literary form to another—from stories to drama to exhortations to letters to explanations or to parables—in a short space of time.

Introductions to the Readings?

A way of solving this problem is the practice of a brief introduction before each Reading. This introduction is *not an explanation of the content* of the Reading before the congregation has a chance to hear it. It is not a time for explaining the debates among Scripture scholars on the origins or editing of this part of the Bible. It is not a time for giving a summary of the Reading. Rather, the introduction sets *the context*, not the content, of the Reading. Its function is to tune the assembly into the Reading so that they become prepared and attentive to what the Reading will present to them and can then listen with understanding. What is said in the introduction is short and succinct. It should not in any case take longer than the Reading itself.

Often what is needed is some *background* to the Reading, a note on a point of geography or history that situates the Reading, a note on a custom that the modern listener may not be aware of, the story or event that immediately precedes this Reading and helps to make sense of it, or the larger picture of which this Reading forms part. Often the introduction will set the *literary context* of the reading. The Bible is a work of literature and this passage makes sense as part of a larger literary whole. Knowing what comes before, and sometimes what comes after, helps make sense of it. It is also sometimes helpful to give the *liturgical context* of the Reading, noting for example how the Reading fits in with the liturgical season. Or, where the Readings are nearly continuous readings of the same New Testament book from Sunday to Sunday, it could remind people of the passage they heard last Sunday which continues on into this Sunday.

The dynamic the liturgical planners seek to foster here is fundamentally the same as that in the Gathering Rite—making room for the Spirit to move among the assembly. The hearers of the word in partnership with the Holy Spirit make their own connections and interpretations. The introduction simply helps them to begin.

The homily

The homily is often the one part of the liturgy for which participants have the highest expectations. When people criticise the Sunday Eucharist it is very often the homily that receives the criticism. A real challenge for the homilist is how to set in interaction the wisdom that already exists in the assembly with the wisdom contained in the Scripture Readings. One strategy is to give over some of the homily time to the people to talk with one another and then to give some feedback. Another strategy is to share the homily among several people. A further strategy is for the homilist to work with members of the community in the preparation of the homily. Reflection and discussion by a group from the community on the Readings for the Sunday can give a much wider view to the challenge 'how do these readings impinge on our lives today?'[4]

In most Sunday Eucharists however the homily time is short and will commonly be presented by one person. Whether it is shared or not, the homily requires considerable skill both in the interpretation of Scripture and in a presentation that engages with the lives of the participants. Probably for this reason there are many books and websites that provide Scripture interpretations and reflections for each of the Sundays of the year to assist the homilist. There are also numerous books and training courses for homiletic skills in presentation. We do not intend to repeat these here. Our focus is rather on two of the more basic issues intrinsic to the homily: What is the homily for? and Who gives the homily?

What is the homily for?

It is worth beginning here by considering what a homily is not. The homily is not primarily about paraphrasing the gospel (once again) for the congregation on the basis that most of them haven't listened to it very well anyway. It is not primarily about telling them stories or anecdotes that essentially do the same thing but in more palatable form. It is not primarily a testimony from the homilist's own life experience. It is not about telling people how bad they are and need to change. We could expect that a homily might include some or all of these, but we suggest that they are not what the homily is primarily about.

If the homilist is not convinced that there is a message here—not just an explanation, not just a story, not just a testimony, not just a reprimand—a transforming message that needs to be communicated as simply and pow-

---

4. An experience where a group of young people were involved in preparation and participation in the Sunday liturgy through a weekly sharing of the Gospel is described in Shane Halpin, 'Praying with Young Adults—An Approach to the Sunday Liturgy', in *The Furrow* 58/11 (2007): 597–602.

erfully as possible to this assembly, the homily may be doing more harm than good. And if the homilist has only two or three key messages that are recycled every second or third Sunday, then again the homily may be doing more harm than good. A series of such homilies may, for example, convince the congregation that there isn't much of any use in Scripture anyway, since if there were, their regular homilist ought to have found more than two or three such messages by now.

We suggest that the key question homilists can most usefully ask themselves in their homily preparation is, What message is there for this assembly in these Readings? Or, more expansively, What message from the Scripture do I have to give to this assembly that is really important for them (and for me) that I didn't already give over the last six months or so? If there is no satisfactory answer to this question, the rest of the preparation, the stories, the illustrations, the visual aids, the humour and the examples are all gimmicks; and will be recognised as such by the congregation. The homilist is here declaring spiritual bankruptcy in an alarmingly clear way.

Like the whole of the Eucharist, the homily is for the transformation of the community into the Body of Christ, into a Spirit-filled people, into a people of God. It is here also that the outgoing, missionary aspect of the Eucharist liturgy becomes prominent.

What the homilist aims for is a transformation of the congregation. Transformation is a change for the better. In the Eucharist it has a threefold focus: a) transformation of the *individual persons* who make up the assembly, b) transformation of this *local Christian community* as a whole, and c) through them a transformation of the *wider society* in which they live. Homilists often treat each homily as an isolated event. But where people are regularly attending their local Eucharist each Sunday it is the series of homilies over a period of years that builds up their Christian understanding and commitment, or slowly destroys it.

Part of the homily preparation is to ensure that this overall, long-term picture is not distorted. It can be distorted, for example, if the homilist nearly always provides a personal, individual interpretation of Scripture that lacks any community or societal dimension. The homilist, in other words, has focused on personal spirituality but omitted the mission of the church to the world. This threefold focus on *individual*, *community* and *society* provides the homilist with a kind of checklist to ensure a broad presentation of Christian discipleship.

What kind of transformation are we talking about here? The homilist can also distort the Christian message simply by omitting to mention over a period of time important aspects of this transformation. Again here, the homilist may be helped by a short checklist to ensure that the transformation presented in the homily is holistic and balanced. This balance can be maintained by noting four aspects of the transformation of people's lives intended in Eucharist—this is a spiritual transformation that has economic, social, political, and ecological aspects. Each of these aspects of transformation forms part of the scriptural basis for the sacrament of Eucharist and each also occurs frequently in the Sunday Scripture Readings.

One of these aspects of transformation is the creation of a Christian community that shares its wealth, which looks after the basic, material needs of its own members, and is dedicated to the promotion of a fairer distribution of wealth in society at large, including the elimination of unjust economic structures. We may call this the '*economic*' aspect of transformation.

A second aspect of this transformation is concerned with unity and love, both within the Christian community itself and in its seeking to promote styles of organisation based on cooperation and mutual respect and the removal of discrimination in public life. We may call this the '*social*' dimension of transformation.

A third aspect is concerned with power as service not as domination both within the Christian community and in the wider society that removes any subjection of some people to others. We may call this the '*political*' aspect of transformation.

A fourth aspect is concerned with an appreciation of the value of all of God's creation and of living sustainably within God's Earth. We may call this the '*ecological*' aspect of transformation.[5]

These four aspects of Christian transformation, the *economic, social, political* and *ecological,* provide a brief checklist for the homilist. Looking back or looking forward over a period of months, homilists and the liturgical planners who provide them with support and critique can check whether the homilies have presented a balanced and holistic message of transformation.

---

5. The most obvious connection between Eucharist and ecology is the very use of bread and wine in the Liturgy of Eucharist together with the connections in the liturgical calendar between the Christological cycle and the seasons of the Earth. But if these connections are never made in the homily, the community may simply fail to notice them. A recent article that expands these connections is Denis Edwards, 'Eucharist and Ecology: Keeping Memorial of Creation', in *Worship* 82/3 (2008): 194–213.

Who gives the homily?

Most liturgical planners follow the practice that the homilist is, with occasional exceptions, an ordained priest with the canonical authority to preach. This means that the interpreters of Scripture are celibate males with their own particular ethnic identity and with a clerical lifestyle. They interpret Scripture through the lens of this lifestyle. This is an exclusive practice in the sense that it excludes from the community the insights and interpretations of women, other ethnicities, and other age-groups, as well as people with other life experiences such as care for children and political or economic engagement in society. This variety of life experience and understanding of the contemporary meaning of Scripture is excluded by the practice of confining the homilist to ordained priests.

In the fairly common case where there is only one ordained priest in the community, the community will hear only one person's interpretation of Scripture each Sunday for months or years on end. The community's understanding of Scripture through the Sunday homily is here narrowed to that of a single individual. This practice also puts unreasonable demands on the homilist who is required to communicate a transformative scriptural message week after week to the same community. Few homilists have the spiritual, intellectual and communication resources to accomplish this task. It is unlikely, for example, that one person has the capacity to communicate realistically all the four aspects of transformation described above. If homilies are often dull, repetitive, or irrelevant, the fault lies not so much with the homilist as with the liturgical planning that makes such unreasonable demands on one person.

Ultimately it will be the task of liturgical planners to seek a variety of homilists so that over time the full Christian message is delivered in all its variety of human experience. For this to be possible, liturgical planners will need to ensure that rightly talented people within their community receive the encouragement and education to be homilists.

The engaged assembly: listening, silence, and communal responses

So far in this chapter we have looked at the lectionary, the Readings and the homily. These are the active ministry aspects of the Liturgy of the Word and are mainly the responsibility of liturgical ministers. What then of the rest of the assembly? The Liturgy of the Word is dependent on competent, qualified ministers, but all of the participants need to be engaged in the liturgy. Are there less individually active, but nevertheless engaged ways, of participating in the liturgy, and what forms do these take?

Listening

When we talk of active participation we normally mean some kind of external activity. But another important dimension of liturgy is what we may refer to as 'engaged listening'. It is 'engaged' because it is not just listening passively, but involves active attention of the body and its senses. It is participation, not just physical presence. One of the tasks of the readers and homilists is to attract this engaged listening from the other participants in the assembly. We may parallel this engaged listening with 'engaged looking' in which the participants attend to the visual symbols of the Liturgy of the Word such as the procession of the lectionary or the demeanour and postures of the readers and homilist. The intensity of engaged listening and looking in an assembly is a good indication to ministers that their ministry is a real service to the community by its own members rather than simply a professional performance that reduces the congregation to passivity.

The silences

Participation is not all sound and noise. From engaged listening the assembly can also move into silence. These silences involve the whole assembly including the ministers, for these are periods when ministry activity ceases and people have time to absorb and interiorise the impact of what they have heard and seen. These silences interrupt an otherwise constant flow of words. They give thinking time, a time for absorption and deepening, a reflection and taking stock. Planned silences also underline the importance of the words that precede them. Liturgical ministers will need to plan where these silences can best occur for maximum impact and how long they should be. Commonly these would be a short silence after each Reading and a longer silence after the homily.[6]

Communal professions and prayers

In addition to engaged listening and silence, the congregation's participation as a whole is externally and symbolically expressed also by actions-in-unison.

---

6. For a description of a Eucharist that is extended to include reflective biblical teaching, personal prayer in silence and group sharing, see Jean-Marc Turnon, 'The Mass That Takes Its Time', in *The Way* 48/1 (2009): 57–66.

The standard actions-in-unison of the congregation in the Liturgy of the Word are the psalm response following the first Reading, the gospel acclamation, the Profession of Faith, and the responses to the Prayer of the Faithful. These are prayers and actions of the congregation as a whole and there are opportunities here for liturgical planners to enhance congregational engagement in them. If sung, they would normally be sung by the whole congregation with some assistance perhaps from cantors or a singing group. A more intelligible wording of a Profession of Faith may substitute sometimes for the traditional creeds. Planners are making choices here that try to incorporate and balance the retention of ancient traditions such as the creeds with more contemporary factors such as the spirituality of the assembly, their age, and musical ability, as well as the particular themes of the Readings and the homily.

The Prayer of the Faithful has become particularly important in achieving active participation. Having seen and greeted *these* people, having heard *these* Readings and homily, having sung *these* melodies and words, what are the needs that we should now address in prayer? These prayers demonstrate the degree to which the liturgy is hospitable, inclusive, and outgoing. An hospitable assembly's prayers include the concerns of the wider world. They are inclusive when there is an opportunity for all the assembly to take part in them and when the ways in which God is addressed range across images not confined by gender, ethnicity, or class. They are outgoing when they indicate the directions of this assembly's mission in the world.

There is a good opening here for prayers from among the congregation where this is acoustically possible. This is the only major opportunity for prayers from the congregation not prepared by ministers. Liturgical planners will want to encourage this opportunity as much as possible. Alternatively, a minister who leads the Prayer of the Faithful can collect people's intentions before the liturgy begins. There can also be a clear invitation for silent prayers in addition to the prayers spoken aloud. The Prayer of the Faithful often suffers from very perfunctory treatment. A sung response, the use of silence, and a posture conducive to prayer are three strategies that help the Prayer of the Faithful to be experienced as a solemn and prayerful climax of the Word.

From time to time this opening to spontaneous prayer may result in unsuitable intentions such as prayer for political victories or personal favours that other members of the assembly cannot affirm. Or prayers may simply be too long, inaudible, or contain inappropriate language. Liturgical planners will need some procedure, preferably private, of dealing with these occasional lapses that does not include closing down altogether the people's contribution to this form of congregational prayer.

Traditionally the Profession of Faith follows the homily. Some communities however reverse this order so that the Prayer of the Faithful follows the homily. This is to maintain a close connection between the Scripture Readings and the Prayer of the Faithful. It works particularly well if there is a silence after the homily. In that case the Liturgy of the Word concludes with the Profession of Faith.

Ministers of the Word

A number of ministries are active during the Liturgy of the Word. These include the readers, the homilist, music ministers, prayer leaders and those involved in the procession of the lectionary if this takes place. We have already noted in earlier parts of this chapter some of the issues and opportunities concerning the exercise of ministries in the Liturgy of the Word.

We proposed in the earlier chapter on liturgical ministries (Chapter Three) that *competence* (having the skills to perform this ministry well), *representation* (that as a whole the ministries represent the variety of different people who make up the community), and *witness* (that the minister's lifestyle is a witness to Christian living) are the main qualities required for liturgical ministers in general.

The weighting of these three factors will be slightly different for each particular ministry. In the Liturgy of the Word it is probably the ministry of reader that will require most attention from liturgical planners. In the case of readers, the primary reason for choosing people for this ministry is competence—having the skills to do this ministry well. This requires both a) that they are able themselves to interpret the Scripture passage, for reading is already an interpretation, and b) that they read publicly in such a way as to communicate the meaning of the Reading to the assembly.

These are acquired skills, and most readers will need education and training before they read in public as well as in-service training as they continue to develop their skills. Since it is unlikely that most readers will be professionally trained before they exercise this ministry, one of the key components of liturgical planning is a long term approach to continuing recruitment, ongoing formation, and a process for retirement of readers.

Prayer leaders need a slightly different skill set. As with the readers they need to be able to communicate well in public. They will also need to convey a conviction about the serious nature of this shared community prayer. This they will do in the way they speak and also in their body language. They will require an attitude of prayer and confidence that allows them to pause easily while the assembly prays in silence confident that the leader is guiding the process.

Conclusions

The Liturgy of the Word is focused on the communication of the word of God to the assembly and the assembly's active engagement in that communication. The inclusive and outgoing features of the Eucharist are particularly important here. Inclusiveness is important in the sense that the Readings, the homily, and the Prayer of the Faithful incorporate the variety of people who make up the assembly. In this way the Liturgy of the Word respects the divine mystery active in all our lives and is not narrowly channelled through the lens of one ethnicity or one gender or one age-group or one kind of professional occupation. The homily, as interpretation of the Scripture for today, is focused strongly not just on the transformation of this community in itself but, along with the Prayer of the Faithful, also shows the direction of its missionary outreach into society.

Key questions:

1) What lectionary is best for reading in Sunday Eucharist, and should the lectionary itself be displayed during the liturgy?
2) What qualities are required of the liturgical reading of Scripture so that it communicates the word of God to the assembly?
3) Is it helpful to have introductions to the readings and what would be the characteristics of such introductions?
4) What is the homily for and who should give it? What potential is there in our community for people other than the priest to give the homily?
5) What are the best options for the communal actions and responses of the congregation as a whole during the Liturgy of the Word?
6) How can the Prayer of the Faithful become hospitable, inclusive and outgoing? What is our experience and how might we need to change?
7) What qualifications, preparation and training, and processes for recruitment and retirement are needed for readers?

Chapter 6
The Liturgy of Eucharist

The Liturgy of Eucharist is the third of the four main phases that make up the whole celebration of Eucharist. In this book we use the term 'Liturgy of Eucharist' to refer to this major *phase* of the Eucharist that stands between the Liturgy of the Word and the Rite of Sending. It begins with the preparation of the bread and wine before the Eucharistic Prayer and concludes with the clearing of the altar after Communion. The term 'Eucharist' on its own thus refers to the *whole* liturgy. The term 'Liturgy of Eucharist' on the other hand refers to that one *particular phase* that is distinct from the Rite of Gathering, the Liturgy of the Word, and the Rite of Sending. Internally, the Liturgy of Eucharist is composed of

- the preparation of the gifts
- the Eucharistic Prayer
- the Communion rite

Preparation of the gifts

This preparation rite in its bare outline is made up of the bringing of the bread and wine to the altar accompanied by prayers. This simple structure is commonly elaborated in a number of actions of the priest—a drop of water in the wine, hand washing, and a series of short prayers. Some of these prayers are in effect a mini 'offertory' preceding the main offering that is part of the following Eucharistic Prayer. To solve the cluttering effect of so many bits and pieces and the two offertories, some liturgical planners reduce the preparation rite to its simplest form—a practical matter of preparing what is needed on the altar for the following Eucharistic Prayer and Communion.

There may however be good reasons for making this preparation rite more elaborate and symbolic rather than simply practical. An alternative set of elaborations on the simple form of the rite involves a procession of members of the congregation (gift bearers) bringing the bread and wine and sometimes other gifts to the altar. Some communities have revived the ancient custom of bringing food to the altar that will later be distributed to the needy. Some communities have also developed a more elaborate procession derived from cultures with significant and graceful ceremonies for traditional presentations of gifts. This is the case, for example, with some Polynesian ceremonial presentations. The *preparation* of gifts thus becomes a *ceremonial presentation* of gifts. Such a liturgical use of a culturally derived ceremony is often impressive and dramatic. It emphasises the people's active role leading into the Eucharistic Prayer.

The preparatory rite can thus be simple, muddled, dull, engaging, dramatic, uplifting, irritating, or some combination of all of these. In its simple form it leads people in a direct and uncluttered way into the Eucharistic Prayer. But liturgical planners should be wary lest this intended simplicity become just dullness or convey the impression that the Eucharistic Prayer is an affair of the priest rather than the whole assembly. In its more culturally rich form, this rite can lead people energetically and intensely into participation in the Eucharistic Prayer. But, again, there is a caution for liturgical planners that such inculturation brings with it the politics of living peoples. Most liturgists are used to liturgical expression derived from the rituals of past cultures, such as the ancient Mediterranean cultures of Greece and Rome, or the traditions of Europe. They will also need the skills of people well versed in the complexities of contemporary cultures when attempting to incorporate the rituals of living peoples into liturgy. This is worth striving for, nevertheless, as it heightens participation if people can bring their familiar cultural symbols into the liturgy.

Liturgical planners, depending on the cultural mix in their communities, have a choice here between a direction towards simplicity and one towards a richer community involvement. A common failure of liturgical planning that occurs here though is that a ceremonial presentation (coming from the congregation) is simply *added to* all the cluttered actions and prayers (by the priest as described above). That is, the preparatory rite is done *twice*.

Liturgical planners are also faced with decisions of practicality and principle to do with the bread and wine used at Eucharist.[1] A concern for high

---

1. And along with this are decisions about the vessels used in Eucharist and its associated liturgies, such chalice, paten, ciborium, pyx, and monstrance, with the potential issues of a theology of speedy convenience. For these issues, see Thomas O'Loughlin, 'The Liturgical Vessels of the Latin Eucharistic Liturgy: A Case of an Embedded Theology', in *Worship* 82/6 (2008): 482–504.

participation would imply that the bread be recognisably bread rather than small rounded hosts and that there be sufficient wine for the whole assembly. There are some practical considerations here such as the manner of distribution and preservation of the consecrated bread in large congregations and the availability or cost of wine in some countries. We suggest though that the objective of recognisably unleavened bread and wine for the whole assembly be regarded as the desirable goal for full participation. The deeper theological discussion on whether local foods other than bread and wine could be used in Eucharist is one, we suggest, that needs further theological discussion before liturgical planners take action on it.

The Eucharistic Prayer: principles of participation

Three foundational principles serve to guide our approach to the Eucharistic Prayer from the point of view of liturgical planning and ministry. The first principle is that the Eucharistic Prayer is about *praise and thanksgiving*. The Eucharistic Prayer may be described succinctly as thanksgiving to God Creator, memorial of Jesus Christ, and invocation of the Holy Spirit. It is a thanksgiving offering for God's benevolence and a prayer for its continuance. (Or more expansively, it unfolds in three waves of praise, thanksgiving and petition).[2] Its overriding tone is gratitude to a benevolent God. Since Eucharist is the most common and regular of the major liturgies of the Christian Church, it also sets the tone for the whole of Christian life: the disciple lives with a thankful heart, and thankfulness is at the heart of the Christian community. All liturgical practices grow out of this fundamental attitude to God.[3]

A second foundational principle for liturgical planners is that the Eucharistic Prayer is about *unity* in a sense that is in counterbalance with the Liturgy of the Word. The phrase, 'the table of the Word and the table of the Eucharist' has become a common one to suggest that both are important. But we need also to be attentive to the ways in which the Liturgy of the Word and the Liturgy of Eucharist are different from each other. They balance each other, not because they are the same, but because they symbolise comple-

---

2. This image is from Joseph Gelineau, *Liturgical Assembly Liturgical Song* (Portland, Oregon: Pastoral Press, 2002), 68.
3. The strong connection between thanksgiving and petition particularly in the Eucharistic Prayer is advocated by Gerard Moore, 'The Petitionary Nature of the Mass', in *The Australasian Catholic Record* 86/3 (2009): 318–127.

mentary aspects of the community's relationship to God. The messages of the Liturgy of the Word may sometimes be divisive and provocative in that they may often be prophetic. They may, in other words, be a call to the community to be faithful and live truthfully in situations where they have failed to do so. The Eucharistic Prayer, by contrast, is a unified thanksgiving to God and a prayer that God will continue to help us in ways about which we all do basically agree.

To put this negatively, the Eucharistic Prayer is not a place for divisive language such as sexist language that identifies either the people or God as male when they are not. Nor is the Eucharistic Prayer the place for the private agendas or moral exhortations that deal with the issues of the day as sometimes occurs when liturgical planners create new Eucharistic Prayers. The Eucharistic Prayer, in other words, carries the weight of inclusiveness of both the local and the universal church. It is the prayer that most needs the common consent of the whole community.

A third foundational principle is that the Eucharistic Prayer is a *dialogue* prayer between priest and congregation. It is not simply a prayer of the priest. Many people in our communities are not sure which part of the liturgy the term 'Eucharistic Prayer', or 'Thanksgiving Prayer' refers to. But they recognize it quite quickly if we describe it as that boring bit in the middle when the priest talks a lot with his hands in the air. This is the part when we can get on with our own thoughts and meditations while the priest carries on with his own, presumably important, business up the front. In a more subtle way, this dissociation of people from the Eucharistic Prayer may carry over to liturgical planners.

The liturgical planners who are not themselves priests may regard the Eucharistic Prayer as not really their business. This is a part of the Eucharist where liturgical planners may need to reverse an embedded 'hands-off' attitude to what happens there. We hope in this chapter to encourage liturgical planners towards the view that the Eucharistic Prayer is not the special domain of the priest but a focus for high participation of the whole assembly in a dialogue form.

The Eucharistic Prayer: words

We have made a point here of these three *principles* of thanksgiving, unity, and dialogue in the Eucharistic Prayer because the gap between principles and *practice* is perhaps greater here in the Eucharistic Prayer than anywhere else in the Eucharist liturgy. We might expect that the Eucharistic Prayer would be a highlight of liturgical participation, but often it is the opposite. Fortunately, there are a number of ways, albeit with mixed results, in which liturgists and priests do attempt to overcome the non-communicative or disengaged atmosphere that often in practice invades the Eucharistic Prayer.

One of these is to enhance the sense of dialogue in the Eucharistic Prayer through the use of *more congregational responses* during this Prayer along the style of the Eucharistic Prayers for Children. A *reduction of words in the long sections prayed by the priest alone* can also help enhance this sense of dialogue and thereby increase the assembly's participation in the Prayer. These techniques involve the delicate matter of adding or cutting out words in the current official Eucharistic Prayers. This requires some skill and communal planning lest the results be just as unsuitable as the current official Prayers themselves.

Another part solution is *singing* the priest's parts of the Prayer in addition to those of the assembly as a whole. Singing in dialogue with the congregation can often engage people's attention in the Eucharistic Prayer. Bad singing and showy solo singing by the priest are common however and likely to have the opposite effect. In addition, what is attractive on an occasional Sunday may be tedious when it continues Sunday after Sunday for months or years on end. Liturgical planners are probably better to avoid general principles like 'the Eucharistic Prayer is meant to be sung' and resort to practical, truthful feedback on the difference between what is beautiful, effective performance and what is not.

A simpler solution resorted to by many priests is to *alter some of the wording* or to *shorten* the existing English Eucharistic Prayers. If carefully done this may lessen some of the awkwardness and dullness of the English translations from the Latin. It can make the language more accessible to people both in terms of its familiarity and its poetic elegance. It has the danger though that it may represent the idiosyncratic preferences of the priest rather than a community prayer. Many of us have seen or heard individually created Eucharistic Prayers that we found worse than the official Prayers. This should not deter us though from still looking out for Eucharistic Prayers in a vernacular style that is both familiar and elegant.

In the long term, a solution to the dullness of the priest's parts of the current Eucharistic Prayers lies in a process by which *local churches create Eucharistic Prayers* in a formal language that is genuinely their own in vocabulary, structure, and oratorical style. The ancient Roman Rite altered the structures of the earlier Greek Prayers, and the Greek Prayers had already altered the ancient Jewish Prayers. This process would still seek some degree of standardization throughout the English-speaking world. It would also maintain the local church's need and responsibility to pray in a language that invites active participation in its own assemblies rather than be tied to a uniform wording across the English-speaking world.

The Eucharistic Prayer: posture and display

So far we have focused on the words of the Eucharistic Prayer. But this prayer is not just words. It is also *posture* (standing, sitting, kneeling, bowing, genuflecting, and facing). Another part solution to the congregation's disengagement is that the whole assembly stand during the Eucharistic Prayer.[4] The unity of the whole assembly in this dialogue Prayer is enhanced if the whole assembly, including the priest, adopts the same posture. If the priest stands while the rest of the assembly kneel or sit, this may signal that the priest is here in a mediatorial role in which little participation is required of the congregation. But liturgical planners need to be attentive to cultural differences operative here in the symbolism of posture.

It is sometimes argued that the whole assembly should stand confidently before God rather than kneeling or sitting during the Eucharistic Prayer—an attitude of confidence rather than penitence or simple attendance. But this is a culturally specific interpretation of standing. For some cultures standing is disrespectful, and for others sitting while another speaks is a normal respectful and attentive posture. Liturgical planners are better not to assume that there is a one-suits-all symbolism of posture. Inter-cultural discussions will need to precede any liturgical decisions.

The Eucharistic Prayer is made up not just of words and posture. It is also quite strong in visual symbols; it is a *visual display* of dress and gesture (movements of the upper body especially arms, head, and face). These visual symbols are commonly concentrated on the priest as prayer leader. Strong colours in archaic vestments along with large gestures on the part of the priest emphasize the priest's solo performance and separation from the congregation. They correspondingly reduce the participation of the congregation when the members of the congregation do not themselves wear elaborate customs or engage in large gestures. Liturgical planners may need to make decisions here about the symbolic separation of the priest from

---

4. A summary of historical precedents for this and recent debates in USA is contained in Judith M. Kubicki, *The Presence of Christ in the Gathered Assembly* (New York/London: Continuum, 2006), 84-87.

the congregation or look for symbols that encourage a sense of inclusion of priest and congregation.

The issue of 'concelebration' by priests is related to the question above of visual display. Priests' concelebrations, where priests wear liturgical robes and stand close to the altar but do not have any obvious role to play there, involve such visual display. The issue for liturgical planners when such concelebrations are proposed is whether or not their symbolic impact may be one of clericalism, demonstrating the hierarchical status of clergy over laity. When the clergy are all male, they may also demonstrate the marginalized position of women in a hierarchical church. Liturgical planners will need to make some assessment of what these symbols are saying to their communities where the impact may be rather different from what the concelebrating priests themselves imagine it to be.

The Communion Rite

The Communion Rite is the part of the Eucharist that most directly symbolizes the relationships of belonging and service in the Christian community. Who belongs? Do some people belong more than others? Could I belong more? Are we all the same? Are we just individuals here accessing divine grace for our own benefit? Do some people serve others? Do some people dominate others? The decisions of liturgical planners are concerned with these questions. Communion with God involves communion with the people of God. Such communion is made up of relationships of belonging and service, symbolized most intensely in the Communion Rite of Eucharist.

The movement towards greater participation in Eucharist that gathered momentum in the mid-20th century was part of a larger movement towards greater participation in the Church as a whole. It supported more frequent *reception* of Communion by church members. It also introduced an active role for community members in the *distribution* of Communion as special (or 'extraordinary') ministers. For many centuries such closeness to the most sacred of all Christian symbols, the consecrated bread and wine, had been reserved largely to ordained priests. The reverence accorded the consecrated bread and wine in those centuries required that people not specially ordained be symbolically distant from them—not touch them, not distribute them, not normally enter the sanctuary, not carry them from one place to another. The most extreme form of this symbolic distance based on reverence for the sacred was expressed in absenting oneself from even receiving the consecrated bread or wine at all for long periods of time. Over the last half-century the movement towards greater participation has lessened much of that symbolic distance and encouraged symbolic closeness to the divine presence.

Yet the consecrated bread and wine are not only the most sacred of symbols but also the most intimate of symbols. They are consumed by the participants and thus enter into intimate internal union with them. The Divine Body enters physically and spiritually into the bodies of the participants in the rite of Communion. This intimacy with the Divine affects the members of the assembly not just as individuals, but also the relationships among them as a community. As the Divine Presence takes bodily form in the bread and wine, that same Divine Presence takes ritual form in the symbolic actions of Communion. The rite of Communion expresses and creates the relationships of belonging and identity that constitute that community.

The Communion Rite: symbols of belonging and identity

More concretely though, how does this happen? How does the rite of Communion create these relationships? A simple way of getting at this is to note how the various degrees of belonging in the community are symbolized in the Communion Rite. In most instances of Sunday Eucharist, the Communion Rite will show these differences among the participants in the assembly:

- those who *do not receive* Communion but do participate otherwise in the congregational actions and words of the liturgy
- those who *receive* Communion
- those who *receive* Communion and *also play other roles* (ushers, musicians, singers, altar servers)
- the ministers who *distribute* Communion
- the priest who *leads* the Communion rite.

We need not read anything sinister into such a hierarchy of belonging. We could in principle go a long way to eliminating these degrees as some more strictly democratic churches have done (who hold that in principle anyone can receive or distribute communion) or make only one degree of difference such as that between the presiding minister and everyone else (only priests distribute Communion). But that would be to create a different Church, and that is not normally the intention of liturgical planners. What is of more interest to liturgical planners and ministers are the tendencies within the Church to play up or play down these symbols of belonging.

When liturgists alter these symbols, or equally when they leave them just as they are, they deal with deep religious feelings and affect community relationships in powerful ways. By way of illustration we can suggest here three areas of contemporary discussion about how the symbols of the Communion Rite affect relationships of belonging and identity in the Christian community.

The Communion Rite: contemporary discussion

One area of contemporary discussion involves the *order* in which Communion is received. Most communities assume a traditional order in which the priest receives first, followed by the communion ministers, followed by other members of the assembly. Yet in most cultures, this is an unusual way of serving food at meals. The hosts don't usually eat first. It is more common that everyone eats together or that those serving the food eat after the others. While it may not have been originally intended as such, the symbolism of the priest and ministers eating first then distributing Communion to others afterwards establishes the ministers as of higher status rather than as servants to the other members of the community.

A simple reversal of order where the priest and ministers serve the congregation first then eat themselves afterwards can be a clear symbol of ministry as service rather than status. This simple reversal of order is, in our experience, nearly always noticed and understood as a statement of service by members of the community. It sometimes provokes objections however from those who see here the priestly status diminished. Liturgical planners need to check here too the cultural differences in meal rituals within their own community which may colour people's interpretation of the Communion Rite symbolism.

Many liturgical planners have not considered the symbolism involved in the order of reception of Communion nor its powerful impact. Opposition to the people-first rather than priest-first order of reception is often on the basis that it is not the tradition or that it is not in the official rubrics. Another negative argument is simply practical: what happens if the consecrated bread or wine runs out before the priest has received them? Sometimes however the negative argument has a more theological basis: the priest (and presumably the other ministers) need to receive first themselves so that they can pass it on to other people. This argument appears, probably unintentionally, to locate the divine presence in the priest rather than in the consecrated bread and wine—an argument that is itself a remarkable divergence from tradition. In any case, the order of reception of Communion is a strong statement of relationships, belonging, and power in the Christian community. Liturgical planners will need to weigh up the arguments for and against.

A second area of discussion derives from a wider contemporary movement in the church towards an increased emphasis on *priests' rights and authority* in the church. This emphasis expects that the 'laity' take a more passive role in the church but an active role in society at large. It expects correspondingly that the priests' authority in the church be symbolically evident in the Sunday Eucharist. In effect this means establishing (usually this is understood as *re*-establishing) that the clergy are closer to divine knowledge and power than the 'laity'. This is effected symbolically by making the sanctuary a sacred place of clerical domain into which the non-ordained may enter only rarely and temporarily. The spatial boundary sets up a psychological and social boundary separating clergy and laity. In this scenario the role of special ministers of Communion also needs to be diminished so that their role is always subordinate to that of the priest, dispensed with when not strictly necessary, and requires no special knowledge or training.

Liturgical planners are sometimes caught unaware in these wider movements of authority and power in the church, but need at least to be alert to the way in which the symbols of their Communion Rite may be playing a part in a larger ecclesiastical or theological agenda.

A third area of discussion concerns who may, and who may not, *receive* Communion. These are issues of belonging and its public expression. The most intense debates about reception relate to people who are members of other churches, people who are divorced and remarried, people who are living in de facto relationships, and people in gay unions. Sometimes public declarations are made about this by priests which state a clear position on who may not receive Communion. More often priests and other ministers recognize that there are grey areas here and in process of change in the contemporary church. The decision about whether to receive or not is often left to the individual person.

We will not attempt here to suggest solutions to these issues of who may or may not receive communion. We simply note here that, while such decisions are usually regarded as outside the discussions of the hands-on liturgical planners, their views on these matters may be sought by members of their own local community. Liturgical planners should be prepared for this. Perhaps even more importantly for liturgical symbolism, the decisions made by individuals who find themselves in the situations described above are often known to other members of the community. Their decision to receive or not receive Communion then becomes part of the symbolism of the Communion Rite sending important messages to other members of the assembly.

Liturgical ministers in the Liturgy of Eucharist

Almost all of the earlier discussion in this chapter affects the role of the leader of the Liturgy of Eucharist. We will have some further suggestions about *leadership* in Chapter Seven which looks more generally at leadership roles through the whole of the Eucharist. The two other kinds of ministry (other than leadership) that play a significant part in the Liturgy of Eucharist and deserve attention from liturgical planners are the *gift bearers* in the preparation rite and the *ministers of Communion*.

The gift bearers, those who take the gifts to the altar, also perform a ministry in the Liturgy of Eucharist. When this part of the liturgy takes the form of a simple carrying of the gifts to the altar, it may still have considerable personal significance for the gift bearers themselves. In Chapter Three, which discussed liturgical ministries in a broad way, we looked at qualifications for ministry, preparation and formation of ministers, and the recruitment and retirement of ministers. In the case of the gift bearers in this preparatory rite, the point to note is that these criteria do not normally apply. An important feature of gift bearers is that they remain closely aligned with the congregation, that is, they do not need the kind of liturgical qualifications that we would require of most other ministries. They need to be 'of the people' rather than 'of the ministry'. Therein lie the opportunities for liturgical planners to involve a wide range of people, families and groups in this role, and especially those who are not personally comfortable in the higher profile liturgical roles.

It is a rather different matter however when the presentation of gifts takes the form of a fairly elaborate *ceremonial presentation* as discussed earlier in this chapter. Such a presentation does then require refined ritual skills by those who take part in it. Gift bearers in a culturally elaborated presentation do require the cultural and ritual skills appropriate to that culture.

In the case of ministers of Communion the points made in Chapter Three about qualifications, preparation, formation, recruitment and retirement do apply though with some obvious adaptations. We proposed in Chapter Three that in general the central qualification for selecting liturgical ministers is *competence* at doing the job, but this needs to be modified by *representation* and *witness*. In the case of Communion ministers this competence includes the skill at gesture and facial expression that makes of Communion a gracious act of a God-bearer offering divine grace to another person. Important too is the confidence and wisdom to be able to react when things go wrong or when unusual circumstances present themselves. A mistake by a Communion minister in reacting to a person presenting themselves for Communion—a refusal to give Communion or an expression of distaste or impatience—can result in nearly irremediable hurt. This requires a deep understanding of Eucharist and their own role in it. It also requires an ability to explain the meaning of Eucharist and their own role in it to other people.

In the case of communion ministers, the qualifications of *witness* and *representation* are as important as competence. We gave the example earlier that a Communion minister whose lifestyle is compassionate brings a quality and immediate authenticity to their ministry that sheer competence does not achieve. This is the qualification of *witness* where the minister's lifestyle is congruent with their role as God-bearer in the liturgy of the Eucharist. Since the Communion ministers gathered around the altar at the Communion Rite present such a high profile to the community, it is also important that as a group they are *representative* of the major dimensions of the community itself, especially culture, gender, and age. This is particularly important because the priest as leader can never do this. The identification of the priest leader with a particular culture, gender and age-group can be a counter-witness if there is not some other way in which the community's diversity is symbolized, especially at that moment of com-union with the divine unity-in-diversity that is central to the Communion Rite.

Conclusion

Active participation in Eucharist has been understood in this book as liturgy that is hospitable, inclusive, and outgoing. Inclusiveness is particularly important in the Liturgy of Eucharist so that the sense of thanksgiving and communion of the whole assembly with all its internal diversity is genuinely expressed in its symbolism. The Eucharistic Prayer achieves this feature of inclusiveness if it has high participation of the whole assembly and expresses in clear, intelligible and poetic language the fundamental unity of the community in its sense of thanksgiving.

The symbolic actions of the Liturgy of Eucharist form in powerful ways the community's perception of its own identity. The symbolic actions of the Communion Rite in particular are the ones where the dimension of the Eucharist as negotiation is most clearly played out. The areas of contemporary discussion about belonging and power as service are negotiations within the

Christian community that become established and legitimated in the symbolism of the community's Sunday Eucharists.

Key questions:
1) What are the benefits of simplifying or elaborating the presentation of gifts that begins the Liturgy of Eucharist?
2) What are the basic principles of planning that underlie the Liturgy of Eucharist and how could these principles be more obviously put into practice in our regular liturgy?
3) What contemporary discussions about belonging and service are symbolized in the Communion Rite; and what solutions could be established there?
4) What qualifications, preparation and training, and processes for recruitment and retirement are needed for Communion ministers?

Chapter 7
Liturgical Leadership

The new possibilities for liturgical ministry in the contemporary Eucharist have made up a recurring thread through the earlier chapters of this book. Ministers are those who fulfil some particular role within the assembly. They actively do something *for* or *to* the other participants. Among these ministries the liturgical leader has the greatest impact on the liturgy.

Liturgical *leaders* are distinguished from other ministers by the overall responsibility they have for the whole or a major part of the liturgy. This usually includes some oversight or coordination of other ministries. For a very long time, this has been the role of the ordained priest, or in more contemporary terms, the 'presider'. In this chapter we look at the contemporary challenges that lie within liturgical leadership and the possibilities for a new approach to leadership.

This chapter is concerned with leadership in the four successive 'phases' of the Eucharist liturgy. Music leadership, which is exercised through all these four phases, is more appropriately discussed in Chapter Eight: Liturgical Music.

The contemporary challenge

As commonly understood today the 'presider' is the single leader of Eucharist who is actively in charge of the whole liturgy. He (currently always male in the Roman Rite) can do all the active ministries himself but is usually assisted by other ministers. These other ministers have specific and limited roles at particular points in the liturgy. The idea of such a 'presider' is a more participatory idea than an older model of the priest who simply 'says Mass', that is, does nearly everything apart from the congregational responses. In comparison with this earlier model, the model of a presider with assistant ministers is moderately hospitable, inclusive, and outgoing depending on the theological views and personality of the priest.

Several problems with this single presider model of leadership in Eucharist have appeared, however, as communities have gained experience with it over the decades since the Second Vatican Council. Three of these are particularly relevant to issues of participation.

One of these problems is the degree to which the liturgy becomes dependent on the views and personality of the priest presider. The older model of the priest Mass-sayer was *rules*-dependent in the sense that the priest, with his back to the people much of the time, conducted his performance according to the liturgical rules which required minimal spontaneous or personalized interaction with the congregation. This was liturgy which valued a sense of the sacred and minimized the personality of the priest. In the new 'presider' model the priest, facing the people, has become a real human personality adapting the rules and interacting with the congregation as well as with other ministers in the sanctuary. The Eucharist liturgy has become *priest*-dependent. It is vulnerable to the priest's personality, to the populist performer as well as to the authoritarian manager, with little to mitigate this effect from the beginning to the end of Eucharist.

A second problem with the single presider lies rather in the nearly impossible burden it places on the priest. The priest is here expected to conduct a Sunday liturgy not just according to the liturgical rules but which is nourishing and formative for the same Sunday participants week after week and year after year. Few priests have the depth of spirituality or the skills of communication to maintain such a role for a long period of time. The consequences of such a demand may be burn-out for the priest and an increasingly tedious or repetitive liturgy in that community.

A third problem arises from the same expectation that Sunday Eucharist be less rules-dependent and more communicative. The single presider works within the limitations of his own gender, ethnicity, age-group, celibacy, professional education and life-style. This enhances his ability to communicate with some sections of the community but severely limits it with others. Even his best performance will be transformative for some but unconvincing for others. Even more seriously, it means that the representation of God and the communication of Christ's message that occurs in the Sunday Eucharist is already narrowed beyond his control even before the effects of his own personality come into play.

A contemporary solution to the problems of the single presider in Eucharist is a model of shared liturgical leadership. It is this model, or some local modification of it, that we recommend to the serious consideration of liturgical planners in local communities.

Shared liturgical leadership: a three-leader model

An alternative to the single presider is the model of shared liturgical leadership, or more specifically, a three-leader model of Eucharist. We have described earlier the four phases that the Eucharist liturgy moves through: Rite of Gathering, Liturgy of the Word, Liturgy of Eucharist, and Rite of Sending. These phases are signalled liturgically by a change of focus, from the gathering assembly itself to Scripture, from Scripture to bread and wine, and from bread and wine to the outgoing assembly. Each phase of the liturgy focuses on a particular aspect of the real presence of Christ: Christ gathering the people together, Christ present in the Word, Christ present in the Eucharist, and Christ calling the people out on mission.

As each of these phases has a different focus and a different purpose, they also have a different style of leadership. These leadership roles need not be filled by the same person throughout the entire liturgy. In a shared leadership model, each of these phases of Eucharist may have a different person as its leader rather than a single presider for all of them.

The Rite of Gathering and the Rite of Sending are shorter than the other phases of Eucharist and clearly complement each other as opening and closing the liturgy. For this reason, it often helps the flow of the liturgy if the same person is leader for both of these rites. Thus a shared leadership model becomes in practice a three-leader model: a leader of both Gathering and Sending, a leader of the Liturgy of the Word, and a leader of the Liturgy of Eucharist. Some local communities may prefer to have a different person leading the Rite of Gathering from the one who leads the Rite of Sending. We shall assume, however, a three-leader model of shared liturgical leadership throughout this chapter.

The leaders of each phase of the Eucharist are not normally expected to do everything themselves. Inherent in their role as leaders is their enabling and encouraging of other ministers in their own distinct roles. The leadership role also includes coping with unplanned incidents that happen during the liturgy such as a last minute change when a rostered minister has not arrived or liturgical books are not in their expected place. It requires partnership between the three leaders. Their joint preparation will give the liturgy richness and depth as well as unity and cohesion.

A model of shared liturgical leadership widens the task of liturgical planning in local communities. Liturgical planning now includes recruitment and training for these leadership roles so that there are a sufficient number of such leaders trained and commissioned in the local community. While the tasks of liturgical planning are here increased, the results will be an amplified and enriched liturgy where, over time, a variety of leaders reflect the composition of the assembly: men and women, young and old of the various cultures gathered. The welcome into the assembly is offered on one Sunday by a middle-aged woman, on another by a young father. Over a period of time, the word of God speaks to us as a young woman, older man, a celibate priest, a married woman, or an immigrant.

Many liturgical planners are so used to the idea of a single presider at Eucharist they are astonished there might be an alternative. Yet the New Testament describes a variety of models of group leadership in the early church, and the Eucharist liturgy itself opens easily and naturally to several leaders. It could be argued that the inculturation of liturgy implies that liturgy take on the political structures of society. The single leader model from Grecoroman and European feudal cultures is now accepted in hierarchical church organization—one pastor, one bishop, one pope. But a similar argument can be made for more contemporary team leadership or collegial models in both church organization and in liturgy. This idea of team or collegial leadership is often now practised in local Christian communities and is the idea that also underlies the model of shared liturgical leadership.

The qualities of liturgical leaders

We summarized earlier, in the chapter on liturgical ministries (Chapter Three), the qualities required for liturgical ministry in general under the three headings of *competence* (having the skills to perform this ministry well), *representation* (that as a whole the ministries represent the variety of different people who make up the community), and *witness* (that the minister's lifestyle is a witness to Christian living). These same qualities are also needed for liturgical leaders but at a higher level and with some additions.

Witness of life is important in leaders since their public liturgical profile creates the expectation that they demonstrate a Christian lifestyle in the politics and economics of everyday life beyond the liturgy. That the range of liturgical leaders represents the variety of different people who make up the community is also an important goal for liturgical planners since this will enrich the liturgy and engage people in its symbolism.

The liturgical skills that come under the heading of 'competence' are however the ones most likely to demand the attention of liturgical planners. No leader can be considered competent without a clear theological understanding of the nature of leadership in the church. This will be part of any leadership training. At the more practical level, two kinds of leadership skills contribute to the competence of the liturgical leader.

One of these is the range of body language that attracts the attention of the congregation. The leader needs to claim attention but not alienate the assembly. This is helped by actions and gestures that are confident and dignified, but appropriate to the size of the congregation and its cultural make-up. Above all, this body language needs to convey the message that the whole assembly is engaged in a liturgical action that they do together.[1]

A second important range of leadership skills is a high level of competence in public speaking. This competence includes the self confidence and mental agility to retain a welcoming style of speech across a variety of both formal and informal situations: from formal prayers, to dealing with the unexpected event, to giving out needed information, to announcing a wrongly parked car, to creating a silent pause, to inviting the assembly to pray.

Also included in these public speaking skills is the ability to use a range of images of God and inclusive language. Our relationship with God and with one another is proclaimed in the images used by the leader. Christ Our Brother is very different from Christ Our King. Both may have a place, but liturgical leaders need to be keenly aware of the very different relationship they each describe. Traditional liturgical images of God are severely restricted with male, kingly images dominating. Liturgical leaders may need to change these and substitute a wider range of images.[2] Adapting the images of God is a sensitive question and requires liturgical leaders and planners to co-operate in thoughtful and open discussion. All the language used needs to pass the test of inclusiveness: inclusive of gender, age, culture and special groups.

In addition to these general leadership skills, each of the three leadership roles has skills specific to that role and these deserve our attention in some more detail.

---

1. With the shift from all male presiders to a combination of both women and men liturgical leaders comes the issue of whether the practices of leadership, especially the non-verbal ones such as standing, sitting, eye-contact, tone of voice, silence, distance, the gestures of the hand, head and body, and their decoration are and should be different for women than for men. This issue of 'gendered' leadership is discussed in Stephen Burns, "'Presiding Like a Women': Feminist Gestures for Christian Assembly," *Feminist Theology* 18, no. 1 (2009): 29-49.
2. Most liturgical leaders will probably be guided by existing official texts in the more complex matter of Trinitarian language: when and how often to address the 'Father' *through* the Son and *in* the Holy Spirit, or to address directly the three Persons whether collectively (Glory be to the Father *and* to the Son *and* to the Holy Spirit) or any one Person alone (Christ have mercy. Come Holy Spirit), or simply address 'God' without any Trinitarian indications. These issues are discussed from the point of view of liturgical tradition in Bryan D. Spinks, ed., *The Place of Christ in Liturgical Prayer: Trinity, Christology, and Liturgical Theology* (Collegeville, Minnesota: Liturgical Press, 2008).

Leading the Rites of Gathering and of Sending

We assume in this section that the leader of the Gathering Rite is also leader of the Sending Rite. We assume too that the leader of these Rites will not always be, but might sometimes be, an ordained priest.

The *Rite of Gathering* extends from the first informal encounters of people as they assemble up to the Collect Prayer. The members of the assembly are themselves the primary creators of a hospitable liturgy and in large measure they will create the atmosphere of welcome and inclusiveness. Also important though is the style of the leader. The leader of this Rite will often be engaged initially with other members of the assembly in informally greeting and welcoming people as they arrive. At this stage the leader may also work with other ministers such as ushers and 'welcomers'.

The leader's formal role begins at the first announcement that calls people's attention to the start of the formal liturgy. This role includes initiating the procession if there is one, welcoming the whole assembly and any special groups or visitors, giving initial information about that particular Sunday, indicating any variations in the Gathering Rite for that Sunday—a blessing with sprinkled water, a different song of praise, or a particular form of penitential rite for example—and leading the prayers such as those of the Act of Penitence and the Collect Prayer. In this first phase of gathering the assembly, the tone of the assembly is set as hospitable and inclusive, or formal and repetitive, or tragically, as a place where social discriminations are treated as acceptable. Above all it conveys the initial presentations of the images of God in whom this community believes and in whose name it gathers. The attitudes and language of the leader play a decisive role in setting this initial tone and conveying these initial impressions.

In this formal part of the Gathering Rite, the leader performs most of the ministry actions apart from those of the musicians. Nevertheless the leader may also encourage here the participation of other ministries where feasible, such as playing a part in an entrance procession or a penitential litany. After the Gathering Rite the leader, as one in touch with the particular style and characteristics of this assembly, remains alert to any needs that arise for the members of the assembly during the rest of the liturgy.

The *Rite of Sending* extends from the Prayer after Communion to the departure of people from the place of assembly. Formally it concludes with the final blessing and dismissal. (In some communities the Prayer after Communion is regarded as the conclusion of the Communion Rite and in that case the Sending Rite is deemed to begin with the announcements.) The leader of the Sending Rite, as well as playing an overall coordinating role, would normally also pray the Prayer after Communion, the final blessing and say the words that send the assembly out. Many of the current official Prayers after Communion simply pray that the participants may be better as a result of this Communion, while others have a more missionary intention praying for a better world. The leader of the Sending Rite may need to create new prayers here that address specifically the outreach of this community into the wider world.

Other ministers besides the leader can also be involved in this Sending Rite in, for example, the announcements that invite people to take part in the outreach activities of the community. Here also, the organizers of those activities can be identified to the assembly. The leader remains the coordinator of these other ministries and this requires judgement about the length and content of the announcements—only some announcement are made here; others are notified in newsletters and notice boards.

Finally this leadership involves the summoning up of a prayerful atmosphere for the final blessing and dismissal. Here the leader may need to find new words that are not as formal or institutionalized as those in the liturgical books. These words do not need to be the same each Sunday. Rather they can sum up in brief compass the mission of the community that has been pinpointed or brought into focus in the earlier Liturgy of the Word or Liturgy of Eucharist. These are the last words, the brief statement that announces the community's outreach into the world. For that reason it is also a prime moment of identity formation for the community.

What qualities should liturgical planners be looking for in selecting people to fill this role of leading the Gathering and Sending Rites? In addition to the general qualities of leadership noted earlier, the specific characteristic of the leader of the Gathering and Sending is that this person is one anchored to this place and this community, and needs to be a person recognized as such by the community. A good leader of these Rites will then be an approachable person with knowledge of the networks of relationships that make up the community, who is involved in the activities and is part of the history of the community. This allows the leader to greet the regular participants, to recognize and welcome the stranger, and be able to introduce one to the other.

In effect this leader acts as host who welcomes people into the assembly. As host, the leader is familiar with the spirit that animates this community, is open to outsiders, but is also able to recognize the kind of attitudes that might violate or destroy that community spirit. This leader has a strong sense of what this community stands for, the tone of its gathering and the directions of its outreach, and is able to communicate these briefly and effectively.

Leading the Liturgy of the Word

The Liturgy of the Word extends from the first Reading to the Prayer of the Faithful. Again here we assume that the leader of the Liturgy of the Word will not always be, but might sometimes be, an ordained priest.

The primary task of the leader of the Liturgy of the Word is to ensure that the Scriptures are made accessible to the assembly: that the people hear and understand, and have the opportunity to reflect upon, pray about, and respond to what they hear. The leader's role is firstly a coordinating one that includes attention to the flow and timing of the liturgy such as the movement of readers, the timing of silences, and the initiation of communal responses where necessary. It will normally include also the ministry tasks of introducing the Readings, reading the Gospel, and giving the homily. Sometimes however these tasks might be delegated to other ministers. Giving the homily, for example, or introducing the Readings or reading the Gospel might be assigned to a person other than the leader. In any case, the first two Scripture Readings are normally read by people other than the leader. Similarly, other ministers normally lead the communal responses and the Prayer of the Faithful.

What qualities should liturgical planners be looking for in selecting people to fill this role of leading the Liturgy of the Word? The qualities of competence, witness and representation as indicated earlier in this chapter for liturgical leadership apply also here. In the case of leaders of the Word, it is the quality of competence that is particularly important. Primary qualifications are an extensive knowledge of Scripture and the ability to communicate with the assembly. Since the leader of the Liturgy of the Word is often also the homilist, this person needs these skills at a higher level and intensity than that required for readers. The ability to communicate may also require different skills for different assemblies or parts of the assembly. The leader who preaches well to adults may not be able to communicate as well with children or adolescents, and vice versa. Liturgical planning needs to take a long term view that plans many years ahead and envisages a future where a sizeable number of its members will be skilled in this role. This will require that people have access to educational programs focused particularly on Scripture interpretation and communication skills.

Leading the Liturgy of Eucharist

The Liturgy of Eucharist extends from the presentation of the gifts to the end of Communion. We take it for granted in this section that the leader of the

Liturgy of Eucharist is an ordained priest and that in normal circumstances the priest's leadership role in Eucharist combines with a pastoral role in the community and a missionary outreach beyond it.

The leader of the Liturgy of Eucharist prays the Eucharistic Prayer in dialogue with the congregation and coordinates the prayers and actions of the Communion Rite. More than any other part of the Eucharist liturgy, this is the phase when inclusive language is particularly important. This will involve changes in some of the official Eucharistic Prayers so that the images and names of God are more inclusive. The language used to introduce the Our Father and images used at the elevation of the consecrated bread and wine before Communion can similarly proclaim an enriched community understanding of God or reduce it to a few narrow images with little contemporary impact. These short introductions by the leader of the Liturgy of Eucharist further provide an opportunity to make brief connections with the Liturgy of the Word so that Word and Eucharist are interconnected in expressing the faith of the community.

In principle all the actions and words of the leader are a sign and a call to thanksgiving and unity. This momentum towards thanksgiving and unity is strengthened when there is a sense that the whole assembly participates in the Eucharistic Prayer and in the Communion. The assembly slides into a passive mode if the priest seems to be performing an action on his own, on behalf of the assembly but without their active participation. Communion itself can sometimes be seen as a purely passive reception rather than an active participation. The architecture of the church if it has a large, high sanctuary with clear spatial separation of the priest from the congregation may further reinforce a sense of passivity in the congregation.

The leader can overcome this passivity and distance by encouraging the participation of the congregation and other ministers in simple but symbolically compelling ways. Maximizing the people's part in the presentation of the gifts, for example, helps to do this. The dialogic feature of the Eucharistic Prayer can be enhanced by increasing the number of simple and sung congregational responses. Participation can also be enhanced by the whole assembly praying aloud the doxology ('through him, with him, in him . . . .') at the end of the Eucharistic Prayer rather than simply the Amen.

In the Communion Rite, the special ministers are not there simply as a practical measure to make Communion more efficient. They demonstrate the cooperative nature of ministry. This sense of cooperative participation can be further enhanced when the special ministers of Communion take part in the breaking of bread and pouring the consecrated wine in the Communion Rite. Its symbolism is further strengthened when all the ministers of Communion, including the leader, give Communion to one another after, rather than before, the rest of the congregation.

What qualities should liturgical planners be looking for in the leader of the Liturgy of the Eucharist? Since the leader of the Liturgy of the Eucharist is an ordained priest, the liturgical planners in a local community often have little say in who this person will be. Nevertheless the qualities of competence, witness and representation as indicated earlier in this chapter are even more significant in the leader of the Liturgy of Eucharist. The leader of the Liturgy of Eucharist needs to be a focus for unity in the community and one who can inspire the attitude of thanksgiving liturgically, pastorally and in outreach. Local liturgical planners and ministers may often need to help their priests to acquire these qualities.

Conclusion

In word and action the liturgical leaders express sacramentally the nature of the assembly as presence of God in all its variety and immediacy. Rather than the single-presider model of leadership, this chapter proposes a three-leadership model that enhances participation and makes more apparent the richness of God present as the eucharistic assembly. It allows that different leadership qualities may be present in different people and in different proportions. It does not require that all these qualities be present in the same person. Active participation in liturgy is truncated if ministry and leadership is always dependent on the capabilities of the single presider.

Local communities may need to adapt the model we have presented here to suit their own resources and to fit with the process of liturgical change that best suits them. The community is unduly constricted if it is not continually identifying and training its own people for leadership roles.

Key questions:

1) What are the relative advantages or disadvantages of a shared leadership model in Eucharist as compared to a single presider model?
2) What are the key attitudes needed in a leader of the Rites of Gathering and Sending?

3) What long term planning is needed to ensure availability of future leaders of the Liturgy of the Word?
4) In what ways can the attitudes of the leader of the Liturgy of Eucharist impact for better or worse on the assembly?
5) What has been our own most significant experience of liturgical leadership that encouraged participation?

Chapter 8
Liturgical Music

Official documents of the Roman Rite over the last century show major changes in the understanding of liturgical music and its purpose. One of these notable changes is the current view that the whole assembly, rather than the clerical choir, is the place where liturgical music primarily belongs. A second notable change over that same period is the shift from a mono-cultural understanding of what constitutes good liturgical music to one which takes into account many cultures, several generations, different genre of musical production, and many different musical styles.[1]

We seem to be in a period of musical creativity requiring astute aesthetic, cultural, and pastoral sensitivity on the part of liturgical planners and especially of music leaders. This chapter is influenced by this wide-ranging and sometimes unsettling mix of innovation and conservation. It sets its main focus however on seeking principled ways of dealing with the decisions faced by liturgical planners on a weekly basis in creating music that enhances participation in Sunday Eucharists.

Music in the Eucharist liturgy

Music is the creator of much of the wide range of emotional impact, the 'feeling', which people take with them from a celebration of Eucharist. Whether the atmosphere is joyful or sombre, friendly or solemn, celebratory or recollected, for example, is in large part due to the music and singing.

We adopt here the principle that the active, vocal participation of the whole assembly in Eucharist is enhanced when much (not all) of this partici-

---

1. For an overview of twentieth century official documents of the Roman Rite the reader may helpfully consult Jan Michael Joncas, *From Sacred Song to Ritual Music: Twentieth-Century Understandings of Roman Catholic Worship Music* (Collegeville, Minnesota: The Liturgical Press, 1997).

pation is sung rather than simply spoken.[2] A sense of belonging and communal energy becomes palpable when it is the assembly as a whole that engages in this vocal participation. Often this participation is further enhanced when congregational singing is combined in different ways and for different parts of the liturgy with cantor, choir, singing group, or instrumentalists.

The application of this principle of sung participation needs to be applied with cultural and age-related sensitivity. The music leader or enthusiastic priest who bullies the congregation into singing on the principle that singing is good for them may be doing more harm than good. It may be better to concentrate on enhancing the quality of the spoken word, or to creating a more meditative style of Eucharist, or simply to wait hopefully for the arrival in the community of the right musicians or singers who can turn this congregational singing into a pleasant rather than painful experience.

Some of the issues in liturgical music are practical and depend on musical resources of both personnel and finance: choirs, music groups, soloists, musical instruments; but also the availability of modern sound technology, overhead and data projectors, or hymnals that aid congregational participation. A basic reality of planning is that the planners and music leaders work with the advantages or within the limitations of their own community resources.

The issues we deal with in this chapter are those that are more matters of attitude and perspective. With or without accomplished musicians, with or without modern technology, the attitudes and perspectives of liturgical planners and music leaders can enhance or diminish active participation in liturgy.

Largely silent and meditative Eucharists will sometimes be planned in communities that put a high value on active participation. These may have very little congregational singing. Active listening and recollected silence, usually called 'interior' participation, are part of active participation. Some Eucharists may deliberately enhance these aspects of liturgy. More volume and increased noise are not the goal of active participation; nor is incessant singing.

Full and active participation, both interior and exterior, is nevertheless our goal in this book. Our comments and suggestions on music and its role in liturgy are guided here by the understanding of active participation in Eu-

---

2. Readers wishing for a more in depth, yet succinct, explanation of the part music plays in people's participation in liturgy may like to consult Nathan D Mitchell, 'The Amen Corner: "Doing Ritual Means Making Music"', in *Worship* 85/5 (2011): 455–65.

charist as hospitable, inclusive, and outgoing. Our goal here then is liturgical music which

    a) projects a welcoming hospitality to the wider community while at the same time affirming the identity of the local Christian community,

    b) is inclusive of cultures, age-groups, and a variety of ministries within the assembly, and

    c) focuses the energy and direction of this assembly's outreach beyond itself into the wider world.

Performance and celebration

A central concern of music leaders and other planners of Sunday Eucharist is the way in which music is integrated with the other elements that make up the whole assembly's celebration of Eucharist.[3] There are temptations that enthusiastic musicians sometimes face and towards which other liturgical planners may need to be both sympathetic and resistant. One of these, particularly for music leaders in the European tradition of church music, is the temptation to want other community members to share their enjoyment of beautiful music by hearing it performed well during Sunday Eucharists. And since liturgy is worship of God, does not God deserve the best in musical performance?

In a 'worst case' scenario, communities with good choirs may have suffered the experience of the choir 'takeover' that largely reduces the congregation to silence. Communities' with good choirs will want sometimes to include the best of traditional church music in their Sunday Eucharists. But overuse of them reduces participation in liturgy especially in those communities that are culturally distant from the European origins of this music.[4] A parallel temptation to perform good contemporary music, using Sunday liturgy as a performance opportunity, can similarly overcome talented contemporary choirs and singing groups.

---

3. A helpful and insightful book that deals with both liturgical renewal focused on the assembly and with practical ways of renewing the sung parts of the Eucharist so that they involve the whole assembly is Joseph Gelineau, *Liturgical Assembly Liturgical Song* (Portland, Oregon: Pastoral Press, 2002). Readers may also consult Anthony Ruff, 'Sing to the Lord: Music in Divine Worship', in *Liturgical Ministry* 17, Spring (2008): 77–84.

4. Readers wishing to pursue this issue will find an extended discussion of the actual historical and potential contemporary differences between 'liturgists' and 'musicians' in Anthony Ruff, *Sacred Music and the Liturgical Reform: Treasures and Transformations* (Chicago/Mundelein, Illinois: Hillenbrand Books, 2007).

Such performance is often enjoyable and edifying for the members of the liturgical assembly but they then run the danger of losing ownership of their own liturgy and becoming an audience. The difference between an audience and an active assembly is a matter of proportion and timing. The issue here is not just of having too much choir or singing group or soloists or instrumental music in an overall sense. Nor is it simply a matter of too much or too little congregational singing. We suggest rather that the integration of music with the other elements of liturgy means that liturgical planners and music leaders

    a) take a 'whole assembly' approach to music,
    b) focus on each liturgical unit as a 'symbolic whole',
    c) express the special characteristics of each Sunday Eucharist.

A whole assembly approach

A *'whole assembly' approach* to music regards the singing assembly as a combination of congregation and music ministers with interrelated roles. Music ministers include not just individuals such as the music leader, cantor, soloist, organist, or instrumentalist, but also groups such as a choir or singing group who are also 'ministers' in this sense. These music ministers, or combinations of them, might sometimes alternate with, sometimes accompany, sometimes sing on behalf of the congregation or sometimes sing for them. A cantor might alternate with the congregation in singing the invocations to which the whole congregation responds in a litany-style penitential rite. A choir might accompany the congregational acclamations in the Eucharistic Prayer by supporting the melody and supplying the harmony so that the whole assembly is engaged in that prayer.

The objective of a music policy is not simply full congregational singing, nor simply the best music by accomplished musicians. A 'whole assembly' approach seeks the best combinations of congregation and music ministers so as to enhance active participation as a whole. This will often mean different combinations at different times according to the progression of 'liturgical units' that make up the Eucharist liturgy from its beginning to its end.

Liturgical units as symbolic wholes

A 'liturgical unit' as this term is used here refers to the smaller rites or sections within the overall organic flow of the Eucharist liturgy. These are identifiable as having their own particular meaning or identity. We can say where they start and finish and often they have their own particular name. The larger Rite of Gathering, for example, usually includes smaller liturgical units such as an entrance hymn, a greeting, a penitential rite or the 'Lord have mercy' litany, the 'Gloria' hymn of praise, and the Collect Prayer. Each of these 'liturgical units', many of which include singing, makes its own contribution to the liturgy as a whole. Each of these liturgical units comes from somewhere, is leading somewhere, invites some particular kind of engagement from the participants, and contributes something special to the overall progression of the liturgy.

A focus on each liturgical unit as a *symbolic whole* means to recognise that singing is just one of the elements that make up the liturgical action. The liturgical action includes also the movements, gestures, postures, speaking, reading, symbolic objects, spatial arrangements and so on that make up the whole symbolism of Eucharist. It includes other ministers as well as music ministers and other actions of the congregation besides singing.

Many such liturgical units have a particular musical identity and an implied musical structure. Each then invites a particular answer to the question, What kind of musical structure will best serve participation in this particular liturgical unit?—in a psalm between readings, for example, or a Communion procession, or the Eucharistic Prayer. The most suitable musical structure will relate to the other symbolic actions expected of the congregation during this particular liturgical unit. Are they expected for example to walk in procession, receive Communion, listen with quiet attention, or sing a set of words? Each of these actions implies a different musical structure. Is the best musical structure then a litany involving a series of varied invocations or petitions with a repeated response, an acclamation of the whole assembly, a recitation as of a psalm with a refrain, a processional chant, a congregational hymn with emphasis on the words themselves, a hymn sung by the choir to accompany some other action of the congregation?

The objective is to engage the whole assembly not just in the singing but in the whole liturgical action at any particular moment of the liturgy.

Special characteristics of each Sunday Eucharist

Expressing the special characteristics of each Sunday Eucharist means that the music reflects the differences between one Sunday Eucharist and another arising, for example, from the themes of its Scripture readings, the liturgical calendar, and the positioning of this particular Sunday assembly within the wider political and ecclesial events of the community. This aspect of musical planning is one that most planners and music leaders are used to and we need not dwell further on it here except to underline its importance.[5]

The purpose of the music ministry is to engage the assembly not only in the singing but in the whole symbolic action of the liturgy. The three principles of a *whole assembly* approach, a focus on the smaller *liturgical units as symbolic wholes*, and recognition of the *special characteristics of each Sunday Eucharist* serve as a basis for addressing issues in liturgical music planning.

Issues in liturgical music planning

Sometimes liturgical planners hand over the music to the music leaders in much the same way as they hand over the homily or the Eucharistic Prayer to the priest. But, while recognizing the value of musical expertise, liturgical planners should still play a role here that is not merely passive but both supportive and critical.

Liturgical music provokes some of the most heated differences within the local Christian community. Knowing that such differences are likely to occur, liturgical planners do best to approach these in a preventive way rather than have to find solutions to heated issues already let loose among them. These are issues, in other words, where liturgical planners do well to have some policies already in place before the issues become emotive and personalized. These policies need to suit the local community with its own internal variety, they may need to be revised from time to time, and they will differ from one community to another.[6]

There are a number of issues that, in our experience, members of the community commonly present to liturgical planners and music leaders. We have selected four of these as illustrations of the directions in which liturgical planners might develop the policies of their local community for music in their Sunday Eucharists. These are problems presented to liturgical planners in the form of:

---

5. Readers wishing to follow up on the use of appropriate hymns in Sunday Eucharist will find an overview of recent trends in Catholic Hymnody in Australia and discussion on scripturally inspired texts for these hymns in Paul Taylor, 'Liturgical Hymns and Songs in Australian Catholic Parishes: An Analysis of Post-Conciliar Trends', in *The Australasian Catholic Record* 86/3 (2009): 277–96.

6. A number of criteria often employed in the process of music planning in parishes are identified in Steven R Janco, 'Planning Liturgical Music: Criteria and Convergence', in *Liturgical Ministry* 16, Winter (2007): 36–42.

a) we can't sing the music,
b) too much choir, singing group, or soloists,
c) a selection of music that is not liturgical,
d) unacceptable or disagreeable words in the singing,
e) too much of the same and not enough new music.

We can't sing the music

This issue is the most basic one and may indicate that the pitch of the music is unsuitable for the congregation, that it is too hard for a congregation to sing, that the style of music is unfamiliar, or that they just don't like it. Sometimes this issue results from purely practical matters like access to suitable music. The test though of the commitment of music leaders to congregational participation in singing is that the congregation actually does sing. Whatever other considerations there are for the selection of music, liturgical planners may need to hold their musicians to this basic test.

Too much choir, singing group, or soloists?

Communities in which this issue is raised can at least be grateful that they do not have the opposite issue where there is no such musical talent and the problem is to arouse congregational singing at all. Putting the issue as an overall 'too much' or 'too little', as is often done, may be to misconstrue the issue. It implies that congregation and choir are in competition. Rather than more or less of one or the other, a music policy would aim for a 'whole assembly' and 'symbolic whole' focus on liturgical units as described above. This seeks a combination of the congregation and the ministers so that in each liturgical unit the singing is integrated with the rest of the liturgical action. These combinations need not be the same every Sunday and they focus the liturgical music planning on the question, What kind of music will best serve participation in this particular liturgical unit?

A selection of music that is not liturgical?

Is there then such a thing as liturgical music that is distinct from other kinds of music? Many community members, including musicians, have strong views on what is 'good' music. And many liturgical ministers, including priests, often have strong views on what is 'liturgical' music.[7]

There has been a long running historical debate about whether there is a specific genre of music that may be termed 'liturgical', and whether there is a clear distinction between sacred and profane music.[8] Today most liturgical planners would agree that there is no particular style of music that is inherently liturgical. It is not more inherently liturgical, for example, because it is Gregorian chant or because it derives from the classical European music tradition, although these might be more culturally appropriate in some places. Some music may nevertheless have associations that make it unsuitable for liturgy, such as associations with political platforms or military propaganda or romantic films and television.

The historical debate about what style of music is properly liturgical has largely been superseded in recent decades by many communities' experience of cultural pluralism and experiments with the inculturation of Christian liturgy. Today the key decisions for liturgical planners relate not so much to the nature or value of a particular musical style itself but the way in which their assemblies are musically hospitable and inclusive. Does the music facilitate the participation of the assembly in all its diversity in the Eucharist? Is it inclusive of cultures, of young and old, of different musical tastes?

Put negatively, does the music make the Eucharist inhospitable to youth for example, or on the other hand, inhospitable to the elderly? In culturally diverse communities, this question becomes, Does the music enhance participation of the variety of cultures within the assembly, not just in facilitating the religious expression of people's own culture but also in expanding their experience of other cultures?

It is unlikely in the contemporary church that music of a single Sunday Eucharist can be hospitable and inclusive of all the variety of people that make up the assembly. The selection of music for Eucharist requires some long term planning. A minimum requirement for liturgical planners is to ensure that one musical style does not dominate every Eucharist every Sun-

---

7. For an historical and contemporary presentation of music in differing liturgical and cultural traditions see Andrew Wilson-Dickson, *The Story of Christian Music: From Gregorian Chant to Black Gospel: An Authoritative Illustrated Guide to All the Major Traditions of Music for Worship* (Oxford: Lion Publishing, 1992).

8. A broad-ranging discussion of this history and its contemporary implications is contained in Ruff, *Sacred Music and the Liturgical Reform: Treasures and Transformations*.

day. Such a policy would schedule the inclusion of music suitable for the various age-groups and cultures in a regular pattern over several months. An important feature of an explicit policy on this kind of scheduling is that it allows open discussion within the community in terms of its inclusiveness, its fairness, and its flexibility.

Unacceptable or disagreeable words in the singing?

While a broad range of musical styles can be suitable for music in liturgy, the *words* of the singing have more stringent criteria for suitability. One set of criteria is theological and is concerned with the messages conveyed in the words of the singing. The second is more aesthetic and is concerned with the beauty and impact of the words themselves as a form of artistic expression.

Like the words of the prayers and homily, a basic criterion for suitable words in singing is that the messages contained there constitute good theology. Liturgical planners and music leaders are not normally in the business of policing theological trends in their communities, but they do at least need to be able to eliminate the worst forms of bad theology there.

Perhaps more importantly and more clearly within the mandate of liturgical planners is the longer term view of what understandings of God and human life are being built up over time in the sung words of the community. It is not so much the individual hymns that are important in this case but the long term effects of consistent messages or consistent gaps in those messages. When liturgical planners and music leaders choose the words that will be sung in the Sunday assembly they are generating the theology of that community. These are the words that people recall later, the words that provide them with resources when they make decisions about their life commitments, question their engagement in public issues, or seek meaning in life's difficult times.

Particularly important in the long term are the images of God and of Christian living presented in singing. What images of God are most prominent? What images of God just never appear? Are there serious gaps like a lack of hymns to or about the Holy Spirit? Is there a history of words that are overly sentimental or individualistic (me and God, or me and Jesus)? In the words of the singing is there, or is there a lack of, a sense of respect and responsibility towards the rest of human society and to the planet Earth? Is there a sense of the Christian mission to society at large or is there too tight a focus just on the church itself?

The second issue on the words of singing concerns more the aesthetic value of the words. The poetry and beauty of the English language (and of other languages used liturgically in our Eucharists) is often lacking in the Roman Rite presumably because much of the English liturgy is translation from Latin. Liturgical planners can play a role in encouraging or requiring beautiful rather than ugly, disagreeable, or banal wording in liturgical singing.

Liturgical planners can assist music leaders by reviewing from time to time the theology that is being built up over months and years through the sung words of Eucharist. They may then be in a position to point out the gaps in that theology or trends that result in imbalances in that communal theology. Similarly they can play a guiding role in enhancing the aesthetic value of the words of their singing.

Too much of the same and not enough new music?

What is the process for adding to the congregation's repertoire of hymns over time? Unlike the musicians who give time outside the liturgy itself to learning new music, the congregation is unlikely to learn new music except during or immediately preceding the Sunday assembly. Choirs, singing groups, cantors and soloists, in addition to their own contributions to the liturgy, are also a means for introducing new music to the congregation. The melody line of a choir hymn today may be the congregational hymn of tomorrow as it becomes familiar to them.

Most music leaders will already have their own practical strategies for introducing new liturgical music to their assemblies and these will differ from one community to another. The implications of the suggestions made earlier in this chapter are that some past practices such as simply teaching new hymns in the music leader's preferred style or new settings of the 'ordinary' of the Mass (in the medieval style of Kyrie, Gloria, Creed, Holy holy, Lamb of God) may no longer suit the needs of contemporary liturgy.

Active participation in Eucharist is more likely to be enhanced when the introduction of new music takes a whole-assembly approach with a concern for the identity of each of the liturgical units that make up the flow of the Eucharist liturgy. The introduction of new singing also gains from a long term view that gives attention both to the need for musical inclusiveness in assemblies with mixed cultures and age-groups as well as to the long term theological balance of the words of the singing.

The four phases of Eucharist

The Eucharist liturgy as a whole is made up not just of the smaller liturgical units but also of the four 'phases' noted in earlier chapters. These larger phases of the liturgy also have their own identity with their own musical characteristics.

The *Gathering Rite* sets the tone of the assembly. In what spirit and with what attitude does the assembly enter into the presence of God? An important element in this is the opening singing or opening music. If the gathering hymn is dull and non-participatory, for example, it will be difficult to turn this around to a lively, participatory Eucharist. On the other hand, a meditative opening hymn sets the tone for a more reflective Eucharist with longer periods of silence. Are there days and seasons when a penitential tone should be emphasised, but other times when a sense of praise and thanksgiving should prevail? Is this the place to retain ancient words and their musical settings such as the 'Kyrie' and the 'Gloria', or are there more suitable contemporary ways of gathering in the name of God?

The *Liturgy of the Word* requires a very different attitude from that of the Gathering Rite. Here the accent is on listening with understanding and the need is for music that enhances people's capacity to attend to the words of Scripture. Ways of attending to the words of Scripture are dependent upon the culture of the community. Liturgical planners are seeking a creative engagement between local cultures and the traditions of the Roman Rite. But the standard rubrics of the official books often have a mono-cultural basis. A focus on the objective of enhancing attention to Scripture may help liturgical planners and music leaders to determine what is sung, what is said, and what combinations of congregation and music ministries are best suited to this phase of the liturgy.

The *Liturgy of Eucharist* again requires a different attitude from that of the Liturgy of the Word. Because of the emphasis on unity and communion in this phase of the Eucharist it is here that a whole assembly approach to music and singing becomes particularly important. The flow of this phase of Eucharist from presentation of gifts, through Eucharistic Prayer, to Communion Rite allows a range of musical structures (leader and congregation in dialogue, litany of choir and congregation, congregational singing with musical support, choir hymn, soloist, congregational acclamations) that nevertheless combine to emphasize the unity of the assembly.

The *Sending Rite* again alters in musical tone the nature of the assembly. This rite is focused on sending people out into their everyday world again to spread the spirit they have encountered in this assembly. In principle, the musical content of this rite is quite short. Once the focus of the outreach for this Eucharist has been established the departure need not be delayed further. Liturgical 'closure' however is relative to culture, and music leaders need to be sensitive to cultural expectations, such as that of closing gatherings with a communal song, when deciding on appropriate ways of closing the Eucharist liturgy.

Qualifications of ministers

Musicians are liturgical ministers and deserve from liturgical planners at least the same attention in terms of qualifications, formation, and retirement as other ministers. There is an opportunity here for liturgical planners to set up processes for the recruitment of new musicians, to create opportunities for ongoing formation and training, and to ritualize the musicians' role through a liturgical commissioning that publicly recognises their ministry and invites their commitment to it.

We summarised earlier, in the chapter on liturgical ministries (Chapter Three), the qualities required for liturgical ministry in general under the three headings of *competence* (having the skills to perform this ministry well), *representation* (as a whole the ministers should represent the variety of different people who make up the community), and *witness* (that the ministers' lifestyles give witness to Christian living). Where the ministry of musicians differs from most of the other ministries is the high quality of the competence required.

Even higher is the level of musical skill, liturgical knowledge and pastoral sensitivity required of music *leaders*. Competence then tends to override representation and witness as the most important kind of qualification. That the musicians themselves represent the variety of the community may not in itself be so important. What is important in terms of representation is that the styles of music do indeed represent the cultural and age-group diversity within the community.

Conclusions

Good liturgical music appropriate to the make-up of the local community and to the particular moments of the liturgy itself is a major contributor to the celebration of Eucharist. We have emphasised in particular how decisions about liturgical music in Eucharist contribute to the way in which Eucharist is *hospitable* and *inclusive*—or fails to be so.

Liturgical music plays a major role in the *transformative* aspect of Eucharist because of the impact it can have on all levels of our sense perception and our emotions. Liturgical music is often one of the contentious aspects of liturgical planning. In that sense it is a key *negotiation* that takes place in and around the Sunday Eucharist. The outcomes of this musical negotiation affect both the way in which the Sunday Eucharist is transformative and its influence in forming the *identity* of the community.[9]

Key Questions:

1) What principles can best serve to guide the planning of liturgical music for Sunday Eucharists?
2) What are the most important policies liturgical planners and musicians need to develop as an aid to preparing for Sunday Eucharists?
3) What is the particular atmosphere or tone that the musicians are seeking to achieve in each of the four phases of Eucharist?
4) What qualifications are required of liturgical musicians and what are the processes a community needs to set in place in order to acquire such qualified musicians?

---

9. Joseph Gelineau notes lyrically that in the end 'the value of sung prayer in common has less to do with the musical notes than with the desire of each person to irrigate both breath and voice, both body and soul, so that the Spirit may seize upon them and make them a river that will flow into the very being of God'. Gelineau, *Liturgical Assembly Liturgical Song*, 64.

Chapter 9
The Liturgical Calendar

The weekly Sunday Eucharist is the recurring ritual which more than any other represents and creates the life of the local Christian community. This *weekly* cycle of Sunday Eucharists sits within the larger *annual* cycle represented in the Christian calendar. The regularities of this larger-scale cyclic time and the events of the ongoing life of the community in so far as these are captured in the liturgical calendar, are the subject matter of this chapter.

The Christian calendar

Time and space are interrelated in patterning human experience and hope. We measure time by the Earth's movements through space—the daily revolutions of the Earth, the monthly phases of its moon, its annual circling of the Sun. And to this we add a seven day cycle of weeks.

The Christian calendar is one of several calendars by which we pattern our lives. Calendars remember events that have happened in the past and prompt planning for future events. They pull significant events out of their place in history and implant them into the ritual remembrances that create our perceptions of the present and future. They relate us to the seasonal changes in the planet Earth and its cyclic movement through the skies. In our calendars we create for ourselves a patterned regularity that situates our individual and communal lives in time.

Calendars are used in a variety of forms by nations, communities, religions and families. Families for example remember and celebrate the weddings, birthdays and deaths of their members. These remembrances shape the values and identity of their family group. Nations and communities celebrate events that recall their foundations and establish their own particular identity as peoples and communities. Religions similarly celebrate the founding people and events that symbolise their fundamental orientation on life. These celebrations keep alive and elaborate their beliefs and values and pass them on to new generations.

The Christian calendar remembers what God has already done for us, especially in the life of Jesus Christ. Such remembering then shapes a vision for the future, a future in which God will do for us again what God has done in our past. The continual remembering embodied in the calendar assembles and reassembles us. But remembering the past is not simply to repeat it. The annual celebrations adjust to new people and new circumstances. They reshape and adjust the Christian community. They help us to make sense of our experience of life in a changing world.

The shape of the liturgical calendar

The liturgical calendar is shaped by its two high points at Easter and Christmas with their respective periods of preparation, Lent and Advent. The liturgical seasons of Lent-Easter-Pentecost and Advent-Christmas characteristically require a good deal of attention and energy from liturgical planners. The fact that the three-year cycle of Scripture Readings on Sundays is also organized around these special seasons with the 'ordinary' Sundays of the year between them, is further reason for this attention to the liturgical calendar.

The meaning of the liturgical calendar with its special seasons and its high points has developed over time in association with other cultural calendars of particular peoples and nations—the Jewish events of Passover and Tabernacles, the Roman mystery religions, mid-winter feasting, the practice of gift-giving, festivals of light and darkness, harvest festivals, celebrations of beginnings and birthdays, and local cosmic calendars of pre-Christian origin.[1] The celebration of Christian events in the liturgical calendar has developed in association with the seasons of the Earth, especially its association of Easter with spring and Christmas with mid-winter, in those particular geographical regions where the traditional calendar was first developed.[2]

From its origins in the Mediterranean and Europe, the liturgical calendar has been transported by liturgical celebrations to other regions of the Earth, most notably to the equatorial and south temperate zones. Only in the last

---

1. In some localities, liturgical planners may seek to retrieve these calendars where they can be integrated with the Christian liturgical calendar. See, for example, the case of the Celtic calendar in Sean O Duinn, *Where Three Streams Meet: Celtic Spirituality* (Dublin: The Columba Press, 2000).
2. For historical background to the development of the liturgical calendar, the reader may consult Anscar J Chupungco, editor, *Liturgical Time and Space*, Handbook for Liturgical Studies (Collegeville, Minnesota: The Liturgical Press, 2000).

few decades have liturgical planners given serious attention to the geographical and cultural particularities of this traditional liturgical calendar.

Contemporary liturgical planners are beginning to deal now with two important issues in their use and interpretation of the liturgical calendar as this has been handed down to us from earlier cultures in the north temperate zone of the Earth. These may be summarised in the form of two objectives for contemporary liturgical planning: a) the challenge of a global liturgical calendar, and b) the integration of the liturgical calendar with other life calendars.

The challenge of a global liturgical calendar

The Christian Easter, following the Jewish Passover, occurs in the spring of the north temperate zone of the Earth. The light and warmth of spring draws life from the Earth. After the spring equinox (when day and night are equal) the increase of the light results in longer days. The light has begun to conquer the darkness. The church has seen in this mix of historical and natural symbols an image of Jesus rising from the darkness of the tomb to a new life represented all around in the new life of springtime. The darkness of death is finally conquered in resurrection—and in springtime.

Christianity has migrated to most parts the planet bringing with it this particular combination of the historical symbols of Christianity and the natural symbols of the north temperate zone of the Earth. In the south temperate zone the experience of the light and abundance of life is the reverse. Christmas occurs in summer and Easter occurs in autumn/fall. In the tropical regions of the planet the experience of light and dark is markedly different again and seasonal changes are related to wet and dry rather than to light and dark or hot and cold.

Christians in regions outside of the north temperate zone have continued the traditional celebrations of Christmas and Easter in disregard of their natural surroundings and nearly without question. The celebrations of the historical events of the birth and death-resurrection of Christ have become divorced from the seasons of the Earth. The harmony of historical and natural symbols created in the northern liturgical calendar then becomes a misfit of symbols. Yet today we have become particularly attentive to our environment, the seasons of the Earth, and the human place within it. Are there ways in which liturgical planners in the arctic, equatorial and southern zones of the Earth can re-establish a harmony between historical and natural symbols in their liturgies?[3]

The proposal that local churches celebrate the liturgical year according to their own natural seasons would require changing the timing of the calendar so that, for example, a southern Easter would then be celebrated in September (spring) and a southern Christmas in June (mid-winter). The confusion and loss of liturgical unity throughout the Christian world that would result mean this proposal is seldom considered seriously. A more likely solution retains the historical remembrances of the calendar (Easter and Christmas) at their traditional times but reinterprets them in the light of the seasons of the Earth in which they occur.

Reinterpreting the traditional calendar[4]

Retaining the annual timing of the traditional Christian calendar but reinterpreting its imagery in terms of the southern Earth's seasons calls attention to theological insights that are different from those highlighted in the traditional calendar.

Easter in the south temperate zone occurs in autumn/fall moving into the darkest and coldest part of the year. There is a dying-off in nature, a pruning of growth, and a returning to roots. This invites a southern reinterpretation of the death-resurrection of Christ in our liturgical understanding. In a southern winter, Good Friday is more immediately powerful than Easter Sunday. The season of Lent is a movement into darkness and coldness, a stripping away of colour and comfort and a conservation of needed energy. The falling of leaves and dying of plants is beginning all around as a force of nature. But the death of Christ that is remembered at Easter is not a natural death. It was contrived by other human beings to suit their own interests.

---

3. An illustration of the problems of a northern Easter celebrated in southeast Australia with its very different sequence of natural seasons can be found in Clare V. Johnson, 'Inculturating the Easter Feast in Southeast Australia', in *Worship* 78/2 (2004): 98—117. Also illustrating how Australians relate liturgy to the natural seasons, is Carmel Pilcher, 'Poinsettia: Christmas or Pentecost - Celebrating Liturgy in the Great South Land That Is Australia', in *Worship* 86/6 (2007): 508–20.
4. The 2009 Congress of Societas Liturgica was dedicated to discussion of the liturgical year in relation to our own times and seasons. Readers will find a number of articles from this congress in the journal 'Societas Liturgica 2009 Sydney Congress. The Liturgical Year: The Gospel Encountering Our Time', in *Studia Liturgica* 40/1–2 (2010).

The Lenten readings reveal the malice of those who plot against Jesus and the weakness of the disciples in the face of this opposition. They remind us of the stripping down and focusing that needs to take place in our own lives, lest we also divert the energy of God into malice and loss of trust.

In the southern Easter and through to Pentecost there is no new burst of life. It is cold and dark. Yet in the cold and darkness, hidden underground, life is beginning to reassert itself. Bulbs and roots are growing underground out of sight of human eyes. The associated image of resurrection then becomes not a sudden and obvious springing into new life, but a slow hidden process whose abundance we can only hope for in trust, and be ready for it when it does appear often in unexpected places and times. We may proclaim Christ as risen at Easter, but a southern Easter reminds us that this may not be a declaration of something experienced. It is rather a promise and a hope. The Easter liturgy may be a celebration of light and life, but this is a communal act of trust. Outside it will become colder and darker and human malice continues in the world around us. The fruits of the resurrection will take time to appear. We live in the hope of future resurrection, but a southern Easter reminds us that we live in the meantime by encouraging and fostering deep growth. Slowly and often unrecognisably, the Spirit is moving among us, renewing us, asserting new life that will in time break out in a future spring.

Christmas in the south temperate zone coincides with late spring/early summer. And again this invites a non-traditional interpretation of Christmas.[5] Advent in the south is a time of increasing warmth and light, a time of colour and perfume. Each week of December new varieties of flower come into bloom and the days grow longer and warmer. The energy in nature is building to a climax and, liturgically, that climax is the birth of a human child, the Christ child. The Scripture readings look forward to a new future, a new hope. The sense of this new hope is paralleled in the season of spring and early summer.

The characteristics and images of late spring transfer easily to the liturgy to provide images of a God of warmth, light, perfume and growth. This sun

---

5. Readers may be interested in just how the 'traditional' feast of Christmas came about before they begin to think about 'non-traditional'. An informative overview of this is given in Joseph F Kelly, 'Christmas, Advent, and Epiphany', in *Liturgical Ministry* 16, Spring (2007): 65–75. The more contentious aspects of the arguments about the origins of the date for Christmas are presented in Susan K Roll, 'What Really Is Christmas All About?', in *Liturgical Ministry* 16, Spring (2007): 76–84.

is not the harsh heat of later summer but the pleasant moderate sun that calls forth growth and enjoyment. And yet, here again, there is the implication of human malice. With the depletion of the ozone layer in the south as a result of human activity, the sun itself has become menacing to human beings, a cause of cancer, unless humans protect themselves against it.

We have used this reinterpretation of the historical and natural symbols to illustrate how this might work in the south temperate zone. The challenge to all liturgical planners is to interpret symbolically the interplay of historical and natural symbols from their own seasonal environment. A southern interpretation will be different from one from the equatorial zones of the Earth. Liturgical planners in the north may not need to change their traditional interpretations, but can at least learn alternative theologies from other regions of the Earth. And even within these larger zones, smaller regions of the Earth have their own seasonal symbols. Seasons of flooding or of drought, seasonal hurricanes or long periods of clement weather similarly are symbolic resources for liturgical planners.

In undertaking such a reinterpretation of the traditional liturgical calendar, liturgical planners accomplish two tasks. Firstly, they reinterpret the events of the life of Christ and the Spirit in our world and display new or more broad-ranging images of God. Secondly, they enhance the ecological sensitivities of liturgy. Here ecology and religion are re-connected especially in those regions where liturgy had become divorced from the seasons of the Earth. Our lives and our liturgies do not stand over and above or apart from the rest of creation. Our liturgical awareness of our planet and its seasons makes us aware of the wonder and the mystery of the divine impulse which holds all creatures in being.

Integrating other life calendars with the liturgical calendar

Attention to the global implications of the liturgical calendar means paying attention to *location*. Location has other dimensions in addition to the Earth seasons. It has family, social, and political dimensions also. There are situations where the Christian community lives at odds with the wider society; when for example it is a threatened or persecuted minority. In that case, liturgical symbols may be more concerned with maintaining their own uniqueness and difference from the surrounding society. More commonly though, there are elements of people's family, social and political calendars that can be integrated with the symbols of Sunday Eucharist.

In discerning where and how other life calendars can be integrated with the Christian liturgical calendar, liturgical planners are doing more than just making their next Sunday Eucharist more 'meaningful' or 'relevant'. There are issues here that need good judgment. Liturgical planners are affecting the beliefs and values of their Christian community by the decisions they make for or against the integration of other life calendars with the liturgical calendar.

It is already common for Christian communities to recognise special events in the history of their own community, such as its foundation or patronal feast, as well as the anniversaries of the deaths of its members, within their Sunday Eucharists. In this way we integrate our own local historical calendar with the general calendar of the Roman Rite.

The integration of some other life calendars can be more problematic. Is there a place in the Sunday Eucharist for other calendar events such as a celebration of birthdays or wedding anniversaries of members of the community? Is there a place for the wider society's annual or seasonal celebrations of cultural events or historic national days? To exclude consideration of such celebrations altogether from Sunday Eucharists separates the Christian Eucharist from the rest of people's lives. Sometimes Christian communities do this deliberately as, for example, in times of persecution or so as not to draw attention from larger unfriendly cultures. Sometimes this can happen simply by accident or by inattention, as in fact has happened in the case of the separation of the seasons of the Earth from the liturgical calendar as used in the south temperate and equatorial zones.

In the more common case, liturgical planners exercise some discernment about which elements of other life calendars can suitably be integrated with the Christian liturgical calendar and with Sunday Eucharist. This discernment involves decisions on three fronts:

a) the problem of crowded symbols,
b) the compatibility of symbols with Christian values, and
c) issues of permission and power.

Issues of discernment

Symbols can become *crowded* when the Sunday Eucharist is a kind of central post office for giving out messages from many different sources: diocesan departments, church organisations, schools, local community events. There is already a strong case for sometimes including other sacraments, especially Baptism, within the celebration of Sunday Eucharist. There is already a practice too of dedicating some Sundays to special and worthy purposes so that we often have an annual Mission Sunday, Social Justice Sunday, Refugee Sunday, Vocations Sunday, Prayers-for-Peace Sunday, various kinds of Children's Sundays and so on.

More crowding can take place with the addition of special acknowledgments of weddings and birthdays of members of the community, along with acknowledgments of cultural and national events. And these can have an unstoppable life of their own. Woe to the liturgical leader who enthusiastically acknowledges the birthdays or the wedding anniversaries of some members of the community but not others! The result of this can be simply *overcrowding* so that priorities are lost and the Sunday congregation simply turns off from this multitude of messages.

Liturgical overcrowding can also have the effect of crowding out the regular reflection on the Sunday Scripture readings that is the theological lifeblood of the community in its Sunday Eucharists. Liturgical planners will need a consistent policy which encourages some attention to other life calendars in their Eucharists, but in which there is also a line drawn to resist this potential overcrowding. Central to this policy will be the process by which liturgical planners engage with the rest of the community in reaching a common agreement about where this line is to be drawn.

A second set of issues that requires discernment by liturgical planners concerns the *compatibility* of celebrations or symbols from other life calendars with Christian values and beliefs. Among the most obviously unsuitable are celebrations of war victories. As such they cannot be included in a Sunday Eucharist. But it may be possible for a Christian community to reinterpret such celebrations so that they become, for example, prayers for peace in the form of 'never again'. In that way the Christian community reinterprets a cultural or national festival for a different purpose.

Another example of normally unsuitable calendar events are those directly associated with political parties or platforms that would show church support for a particular political organisation. On the other hand though, there could be good reasons for liturgical inclusion of such calendar events as Mother's Day or Father's Day if the commercialism associated with these can be avoided. Similarly there could be good reason for liturgical acknowledgement of annual days that celebrate national identity without partisanship, or of the religious events celebrated by neighbours and friends of other religions.

In making these decisions liturgical planners are creating community identity and establishing their community's outlook on the rest of society, where it agrees and where it disagrees with the values of the wider society. Decisions will be different from one local community to another. What is important again here, as in the case of dealing with overcrowded symbols, is that liturgical planners develop a policy on these issues rather than fall into inattention or be caught by decisions made on-the-run by priests or other community leaders. And again of overwhelming importance in all this, is the process by which the liturgical planners and the community as a whole reach common agreements.

A third set of issues is concerned with *permission and power* in liturgy. Liturgy is an arena vulnerable to the abuse of power. Eucharist is a conventional ritual in the sense that people take part in it on the basis of certain expectations of what can legitimately happen there. There are boundaries to what liturgical leaders can legitimately do there. And there are areas of legitimate innovation which the assembly grants to its leaders. Liturgical leaders need to be wary of possible liturgical abuse that makes public requirements of people to which those people have never agreed or given their permission. If a couple are named and asked to come to the front for a special blessing for their wedding anniversary, for example, who gave permission for this or what agreed process preceded this public event? If someone is prayed for publicly because of an illness, is this an invasion of privacy or again who gave permission for this? Was it given by the people so singled out in the liturgy, by a community process, or did the liturgical leader simply assume a right to do this?

Liturgical planners and ministers who do not feel the need for permissions from above (from central church authorities) in order to add or alter liturgical practices, need to be careful that they do have permissions from below, that is, from the potential victims of insensitive liturgical leadership. Again, the key to dealing with these issues of permission and power is a transparent and communal process by which such liturgical changes are made.

The strategies for integrating liturgical symbols

Globalizing the liturgical calendar to include the variations of Earth's seasons and integrating other life calendars into it mean a change in the symbols of Eucharist. What strategies are available to liturgical planners to accomplish this integration that at the same time maintain the overall integrity of Eucharist as a coherent liturgy in its own right?

Words, movement, and visual object symbols are the three sets of symbols that can most easily be adjusted to achieve such integration. These allow variations to be introduced without violating the overall phasing and flow of the Sunday Eucharist.

Altering the *words* of the liturgy is a strategy that requires little more than attention and sensitivity of liturgical leaders to the Earth and other life calendars within an agreed policy. This means that the words of Gathering and Sending, the collect prayers, the prayers of intercession, the blessings, and the homily in particular make explicit reference to the interplay of calendar events with the celebration of Eucharist. Provided issues of permission and power have already been dealt with, this requires little extra from liturgical leaders except attention and sensitivity.

Altering the *movements* of the traditional liturgy does usually mean additions to traditional symbols. Remembrances such as birthdays or anniversaries can be acknowledged by people standing or coming forward to the centre of the church or being included in an already existing procession. Special objects associated with cultural festivals can also be included in processions and displayed during the Eucharist. Movements are usually accompanied by words either in the form of prayers or by way of explanation.

Visual symbols are also part of the repertoire for liturgical planners. In addition to the standard visual symbols of Eucharist (Bible, bread, wine; also candles, books, cross) and permanent visual symbols in the church (pictures, statues, stained glass windows, light created by the architectural form of the church), temporary visual symbols created for particular seasons or particular events can transmit important messages without overcrowding the symbolic action. Such symbols may include, for example, seasonal flowers or wreaths, cultural decorations, art work, or symbols that mark cultural, national or seasonal events and interpret them within the liturgical calendar. Banners can be particularly effective for special seasons and Sundays dedicated to special issues. A banner, for example, that announces 'Jesus was a refugee' on a special Sunday for refugees carries a strong message with few words.

Local liturgical planners may find it both helpful and time-saving in the long run if they construct their own annual, local liturgical calendar that marks not only the traditional liturgical seasons and celebration but that also marks in other local festivities and events at their appropriate times. This simplifies future planning especially when the planners themselves lead busy lives or when different people take responsibility for the different Sundays of the year.

The sanctoral calendar: the remembrance of saints

Finally in this consideration of the liturgical calendar, we may note briefly the possibilities inherent in the recurring remembrances of saints that are traditionally part of the calendar. Along with the major focus on the events of Christ and the Spirit, the liturgical calendar traditionally includes also a 'sanctoral' cycle, the remembrance of the saints that is principally a weekday rather than a Sunday cycle. This sanctoral cycle, like the main liturgical calendar, is also ready to develop a sense of location that expands beyond the Mediterranean and European worlds.

Keeping alive the stories of foundations and founders, of prophets and contemplatives, of religious and social movements that have formed the current identity of the local community, and role models who provide living examples of Christian commitment, is important for the identity of a local church. In some places local Churches are amending their calendars to include such local lives and events that remind the Christian community of its identity and challenge it to engagement in the wellbeing of the wider society.

Conclusion

The weekly Sunday celebration of Eucharist sits within the larger timeframe of the liturgical calendar. The founding events of Christianity, the seasons of the Earth, and other recurring family, cultural and national celebrations can be reinterpreted within the liturgical calendar. This is a new task particularly for local communities outside the earlier centres of Christianity where the traditional liturgical calendar was first developed. When this task is undertaken with a discernment that avoids the risks of overcrowded symbols in Sunday Eucharist, of symbols incompatible with Christian values, and of the liturgical abuse of power, such an integrated calendar can enhance the identity of the Christian community along with its links into the life of the wider society and of the Earth itself.

Key Questions:

1) How do the Earth's seasons influence our understanding of Lent-Easter and Advent-Christmas?
2) What elements of family, cultural, or national calendars could beneficially be integrated with the liturgical calendar?
3) How can issues of overcrowded symbols, incompatible symbols, or issues of permission and power be identified and addressed?
4) What strategies for integrating other calendars into the symbols of Eucharist are known to work well?

Chapter 10
Related Liturgies

This chapter is concerned with liturgies which are related quite closely to the Sunday Eucharists of a local community. They can be alternatives to Eucharist in particular circumstances, or they extend the symbols and meanings of Sunday Eucharists in other liturgical forms. The ones considered here as most likely to require attention from liturgical planners are Liturgies of Word and Communion, stand-alone Liturgies of the Word, weekday Eucharists, and some liturgical extensions of Eucharist. The chapter concludes with some considerations on non-eucharistic devotions and on non-liturgical gatherings of the local community in so far as these relate to Eucharist.

Liturgies other than Eucharist (Baptism, Marriage, Anointing of the Sick, etc.) that have the status of sacraments would require special treatment in their own right and are not considered here even though they are all interrelated in the overall sacramental system of the church.[1]

Liturgies are interrelated

Liturgical planners often work under pressure of time. This can create a temptation to deal only with Sunday Eucharists without paying much attention to what is going on to the right and left of them or before and after them. Yet Sunday Eucharists are not isolated gatherings unaffected by the other liturgies of that community. Liturgies constitute a kind of language in that they are made up of an overlapping range of symbols. They employ symbol systems of gesture, posture, furniture, use of space, movement, dress,

---

1. A recent overview of the sacraments that brings together psychological, sociological, ritual studies, and historical dimensions of sacraments along with their relationship to morality and spirituality is contained in Joseph Martos, *The Sacraments: An Interdisciplinary and Interactive Study* (Collegeville, Minnesota: Liturgical Press, 2009).

spoken words, and symbolic objects in different combinations to create the particular meanings of each liturgy.

A stand-alone Liturgy of the Word, for example, uses all the above symbol systems in some way or another, but its particular focus is on the spoken word. Benediction of the Reserved Sacrament, by contrast, while it still uses all the other symbol systems in lesser ways, has a particular focus on the visual display of the consecrated host. Good Friday ceremonies again use all the above systems but focus on a particular set of words, the Gospel Reading of the passion and death of Jesus, and on the visual display of a cross.

Because these liturgies derive from a common language of liturgical symbols they affect one another in several ways. Ideally this relationship is a cooperative and complementary one in the sense that such liturgies restate some of the central Christian messages of Eucharist but also display the varieties of that message in different life circumstances. A liturgy of Communion of the Sick in the sick person's home or in a hospital, for example, is intended to convey the Eucharistic message of thanksgiving and trust in a compassionate God as related to the particular circumstances of illness. Liturgical planners need sometimes to take an overall view of how the liturgies related to Eucharist in their local community reinforce, collaborate with, extend, and enhance the central messages of Eucharist. Liturgies like Benediction or Communion of the Sick or the Morning Prayer of the Church are intended as complementary to celebrations of Eucharist.

Many local communities throughout the world are not able to celebrate weekly Sunday Eucharists in their own locality because they lack an ordained priest. The most likely type of liturgy that will then substitute for Eucharist in the Sunday assembly is either a Liturgy of Word and Communion or simply a Liturgy of the Word (without Communion).

Liturgy of Word and Communion

A Liturgy of Word and Communion is in a sense an abnormal liturgy in that it is a liturgy created to cope with the abnormal situation where there is no ordained priest available and, because of that circumstance, a full Eucharist is not considered possible. This liturgy then is an adaptation to a situation that ideally should not occur in the church at all, but does in fact occur in many local communities. In this liturgy the assembly is essentially the same as the assembly that would normally gather for a Sunday Eucharist. The Gathering and Sending Rites and the Liturgy of the Word are substantially the same as in Eucharist. Instead of a Liturgy of Eucharist, however, there is simply a

Communion Rite without a Eucharistic Prayer. The Communion Rite uses consecrated bread from a previous Eucharist of that local community.

Liturgical planners may need to exercise some caution here and be careful about the attitudes they are creating in this unusual liturgy. A liturgy intended to deal with an abnormal situation can become simply an aberration if it is treated as normal. On the other hand it can also create opportunity that is unthought-of when all is running normally.

Major liturgies often create subsidiary liturgies that extend that major liturgy into later times and other places. Communion of the Sick is such a liturgy that extends the impact of Eucharist to a sick person who cannot be in the place where Eucharist is celebrated. The reservation of consecrated bread for a later Holy Hour or for Benediction or for visitation and prayer are subsidiary liturgies that allow some of the impact of Eucharist to be extended beyond the time of the Eucharist celebration itself. There is the possibility that such subsidiary liturgies lose their intimate dependent relationship with the Eucharist and appear to be liturgies in their own right. Such was the case, for example, with adoration of the Blessed Sacrament which often substituted for receiving Communion in the late medieval period in Europe and which the Second Vatican Council sought to reform.

The Communion Rite in a Liturgy of Word and Communion is a continuity of a previous Eucharist. As that time gap between the two increases liturgical planners can rightly become uneasy that the continuity is being lost and that the consecrated bread has become symbolically separated from its place within the action of a thanksgiving sacrificial meal. The same symbolic distancing occurs when the consecrated bread is brought in from a different local community.

A short rule of thumb for liturgical planners is that the consecrated bread shared in a Liturgy of Word and Communion needs to be expressly and obviously in continuity with an earlier Eucharist of that community, or, in the circumstances of no local Eucharist at all, brought in from another closely related community.

Liturgy of Word and Communion: planning

A primary principle for liturgical planning of a Liturgy of Word and Communion can be expressed in two parts. *Firstly*, we can expect the Gathering and Sending Rites and the Liturgy of the Word to look very much like what the community is used to in its Sunday Eucharists. This is after all a Sunday assembly of the Christian community and these phases are normal in most major liturgical gatherings of the Christian community. *But also*, the Communion Rite should look like a liturgical extension of a previous Eucharist rather than a liturgy in its own right. This is fairly easy to accomplish if the normal Eucharists of the community involve full participation as we have described it in earlier chapters of this book. In the Communion Rite of a Liturgy of Word and Communion, by contrast, there is no procession of gifts, there is no dialogic Eucharistic Prayer, the consecrated bread is taken from the tabernacle, there is no consecrated wine, there are fewer communion ministers, and distribution of communion is much shorter than usual. The symbols are all there for the assembly to see that this is not Eucharist as such but a much simplified extension of their previous Eucharist.

This will be easier to accomplish if the normal Eucharists themselves involve full participation. If the regular Eucharists of that community are led by a single presider with only basic communal responses, no procession of bread and wine from the congregation, a fairly dull Eucharistic Prayer without sung responses, Communion is without consecrated wine and with hosts taken from the tabernacle, then people may not notice much difference. The problem then that the liturgical planners will need to deal with lies not in their Liturgies of Word and Communion but in the impoverished symbolism of their Eucharists.

If liturgies of Word and Communion are liturgies designed to cope with an abnormal situation and are vulnerable to misunderstanding, they are also opportunities for creativity. The plan of a Liturgy of Word and Communion looks quite like a Eucharist without a Eucharistic Prayer. In action however, a Liturgy of Word and Communion develops its own dynamic and its own impact. Liturgical planners and ministers need to capture this particular liturgical spirit and the new opportunities inherent in it rather than regard it as a truncated Eucharist.

One of the creative possibilities here is in ministry and leadership. Liturgies of Word and Eucharist are less bound by official regulations than Eucharists. There is room here for creativity that does not involve the wider implications and regulations surrounding Eucharist. Some communities are reluctant to follow a three-leadership pattern or to introduce more culturally sensitive styles in their Eucharists because these are not sanctioned in the official liturgical books. There are few such obligations in Liturgies of Word and Communion.

With adequate training, a three-leadership pattern for Liturgies of Word and Communion relieves the burden of the single 'lay' presider who does everything. It also allows a variety of different talents to surface within the community. It allows the development of ministers who are particularly suited to gathering the community, who are able to give a Scripture reflection, who are gifted in liturgical prayer, who bring a sense of communion in Christ to the community. Much of the discussion and suggestions in previous chapters on Sunday Eucharists can be applied to the Liturgy of Word and Communion except for those comments that relate directly to the Eucharistic Prayer.

The creative opportunities of Liturgies of Word and Communion lie firstly in the way they provide a partial solution to the inaccessibility of Eucharist for many local communities. They also contain creative possibilities for the future in their potential to give scope and encouragement to new and energetic ministries in the church which can then have a flow-on effect to more active participation in the Eucharist itself.

Liturgy of the Word only

Another alternative for a Sunday gathering of the local community when a Eucharist is not possible is a Liturgy of the Word. This can take a large variety of forms including a liturgy similar to the Liturgy of the Word in Eucharist (together with a Gathering and a Sending Rite). Other common liturgies of the Word are the Morning or Evening Prayer of the church focused on the psalms, and more contemporary forms of multi-media worship. In all of these, liturgical planners can be less constrained by official rubrics and responsibilities to the universal church and can be more focused on the needs and styles of communication of the local community.

Sometimes this Liturgy of the Word form is preferred to a Liturgy of Word and Communion because of the ambiguities surrounding the use of consecrated bread from a previous Eucharist, or because of the possibility of people regarding Eucharist and Liturgy of Word and Communion as more or less the same. On the other hand, Liturgies of the Word on their own can seem bland and passive to people who value Communion, and, liturgically speaking, they lack the action, commitment and negotiation inherent in a Communion Rite. Liturgical planners will need to balance these arguments for or against a Liturgy of the Word. It is also possible to add a community action such as a more prolonged exchange of peace or some communal use of water or oil that adds a layer of more active symbolism to the liturgy of the Word. In any case, Catholic communities can here be guided and enriched by familiarity with the contemporary worship of those Protestant churches who have maintained a tradition of Sunday worship in the style of a liturgy of the Word rather than of Eucharist.

Weekday liturgies

Weekday Eucharists are usually smaller than Sunday Eucharists and for this reason have a somewhat different impact on the local community. With smaller numbers of people, possibly catering for different sections of the larger local community, weekday Eucharists enable a larger variety of liturgical styles. Depending upon the kind of people who are regular participants, weekday Eucharists can be more meditative with more emphasis on silence and less vocal participation. On the other hand weekday Eucharists can include more participation in the form of invitations to contribute to Scripture reflection or the Prayer of the Faithful than is often possible in large Sunday gatherings.

Weekday liturgies may not always be Eucharists. Liturgies of the Word with or without Communion are also possible alternatives. What we have noted above on Liturgies of the Word and Liturgies of Word and Communion on Sundays can be applied also, with appropriate adjustments, to weekdays.

Liturgical planners are unlikely to give the same amount of attention to weekday liturgies as they do to the major Sunday assemblies. Two features of weekday liturgies may be helpful in guiding the attention liturgical planners give to these liturgies. *Simplicity* is often a desirable feature of weekday liturgies so that ministers can follow a relatively regular pattern that does not require constant planning and does not result in the liturgical exhaustion that sometimes overcomes liturgical planners. When there are fewer available ministers on weekdays, the patterns of ministry and leadership can also be simplified. Instead of a three-leadership pattern, for example, weekday Eucharists or Liturgies of Word and Communion may simplify to a two-leadership pattern (one leads the Gathering and Word, the other leads the Liturgy of Eucharist or Communion Rite and the Sending Rite), or simply fall back on a single leader for the whole liturgy.

Another feature of weekday liturgies is the possibility there for *apprenticeship* and *experiment*. Weekday liturgies do not carry the same weight or power as Sunday Eucharists. When they are small gatherings, they allow inexperienced ministers to take the first steps in ministry that might be too overwhelming for them in a Sunday assembly. A small weekday liturgy with familiar people may overcome the problems of public performance. Similarly, other ministers can learn by experience during smaller weekday liturgies before they take on that ministry in larger Sunday gatherings. Weekday liturgies can also be the first setting for changes in the actions of the congregation—changes in times for standing or kneeling, changes in ways of distributing or receiving Communion, the introduction of local cultural symbols—where they can be practiced and evaluated before they are introduced into the Sunday Eucharists.

Liturgical extensions of Eucharist

Communion of the Sick, and prayers and processions focused on the Reserved Sacrament are the most common liturgical extensions of Eucharist beyond the time and place of the Eucharist celebration itself. Communion of the Sick deserves the careful attention of liturgical planners because it extends the Eucharist to those who cannot otherwise be participants in the celebration of Eucharist itself and who are vulnerable to careless disregard. Where there is a history of brief celebrations of this liturgy by priests under pressure of time, liturgical planning may concentrate on ensuring that there are sufficient, well skilled ministers who can celebrate this liturgy in a way that expresses care and sensitivity for the specific needs of people who are home- or hospital-bound whether for a short time or permanently.

Prayer before the Reserved Sacrament is often personal and contemplative. Where it takes the form of communal liturgies or processions, liturgical planners may need to be sensitive to the different needs and styles of a variety of cultures and a variety of religious personalities. A rule of thumb for liturgical planners is that these are subsidiary liturgies that should reinforce, collaborate with, extend, and enhance the impact and meaning of Eucharist rather than overshadow it.

Non-eucharistic devotions

In many local communities there are also popular devotions with no express relationship to Eucharist. These are often the devotions of particular sodalities within the church, associated with spiritual movements, or a result of local visionaries. It is often the case that the liturgical planners of the local community are not expected to be involved in these devotions and may not even be welcome there. Yet such devotions do affect the life of the community and liturgical planners cannot completely ignore them.[2]

---

2. A helpful commentary that notes strengths and weaknesses of a 2001 Directory on popular piety and liturgy issued by the Congregation for Divine Worship and the Discipline of the Sacraments is given by Joyce Ann Zimmerman, "Directory on Popular Piety and the Liturgy: Principles and Guidelines," *Liturgical Ministry* 17, Spring (2008): 92-96.

The key principle here is that these devotions be cooperative and complementary to the Eucharist and other major church liturgies. This cooperative ideal is not always the case and some popular devotions can take on an exclusive intensity that is competitive rather than cooperative with other liturgies of the local community. This competitive character may be competition for members where people are called to be loyal to one kind of devotion rather than others; or it may take the form of competition among beliefs where the message of one kind of devotion is said to be more effective or more orthodox than others.[3]

Liturgical planners are faced with two issues here. One is an issue of discernment where they need to decide whether they are faced here with real competition implying that there can only be winners and losers. If this is the case, the result may be a decision to exclude or discourage this form of communal devotion. The second issue is a cultural or generational one, where liturgical planners face the possibility that their own spirituality is monocultural or single-generational or sexist. If their liturgical planning is itself a result of such an exclusive, narrow spirituality, alternative popular devotions may here be demonstrating a need for a rethink of the current liturgical planning and ministry.

Non-liturgical gatherings

The Christian community, or parts of it, also gathers in many ways that are non-liturgical. Meetings, social events, celebrations of various kinds, combined actions for social justice or environmental concern, lectures and seminars, and sports gatherings are all contributors to creating a community spirit. They also convey messages that may be similar to or contrary to those expressed in the liturgical gatherings. In that sense they cooperate or compete with the beliefs and values expressed in the Sunday Eucharists and related liturgies.

Such gatherings are usually considered outside the focus of liturgical planners and ministers. When these gatherings are clearly cooperative with Sunday Eucharist in that they enhance the community spirit and implement the beliefs and values enshrined there, they probably need not concern liturgical planners. Liturgical ministers could usefully point out however the cooperative and complementary nature of such gatherings from time to time.

---

3. A good example of the attempt at integration of eucharistic worship and religious popular practices is contained in Roberto S Goizueta, 'Challenges of/to the U.S. Latino/a Liturgical Community', in *Liturgical Ministry* 16, Summer (2007): 124–132.

What will concern liturgical planners is when these other gatherings are in competition with the community's liturgies especially its Sunday Eucharists. Again this competition can take the form of competition for participants as can be the case of sports or school fairs on Sunday mornings. Or it may take the form of contradictory beliefs and values, such as when a community's tradition of welcome and hospitality in its Sunday Eucharists is at odds with that same community's authoritarian style of meetings and decision-making. The opposite can also occur when a community holds social occasions to develop a spirit of friendship but its Eucharists are cold and formal. Or similarly, when a community's actions for social justice are quite unrecognised in its Sunday Eucharists so that a stranger taking part in their Eucharist could leave it completely unaware of any such action.

The Eucharist, especially the Sunday Eucharist, is considered the 'summit' and 'source' of the community's life. Liturgical planners can help this become a reality if, in addition to their major focus on the liturgies themselves, they also maintain a wider view that is alert to unity and diversity in the wider non-liturgical gatherings of the community. They may be able to detect the beginnings of competition or conflict in the community and incorporate solutions into their liturgical planning.

Conclusion

The liturgies related to Eucharist discussed in this chapter are not as powerful in their impact on the community as are Sunday Eucharists. When these liturgies take the place of Eucharist as the community's Sunday liturgy however, liturgical planners will need to give them the same attention as they would for a Sunday Eucharist. The way in which a non-eucharistic Sunday liturgy communicates beliefs and values, impacts on the life of the participants, shapes the relationships among them, and forms the identity of the community is similar to that of Sunday Eucharist. If the alternative liturgy is unusual and has needed to be thought out in a new way, its impact may be even more intense than a regular Sunday Eucharist.

Liturgical planners can be more relaxed however about weekday liturgies which normally do not have the same impact as Sunday assemblies. Here a more relaxed simplicity and the possibility of apprenticeship and experiment can characterise liturgical planning. Often liturgical planners are not directly involved in non-eucharistic devotions many of which have their own devotional patterns. Nor are liturgical planners as such often involved in non-liturgical gatherings. What we suggest in these cases is a liturgical overview that looks for unity in diversity, and in that spirit encourages cooperation and complementarity rather than competition.

Key questions:

1) In what ways are all the community's liturgies interrelated so that each one impacts on the others?
2) Liturgies of Word and Communion are, in a sense, abnormal liturgies, but in what ways can they be either misleading on the one hand or an opening for new opportunities on the other?
3) What are the features of weekday liturgies that make them different from Sunday Eucharist?
4) What attention should liturgical planners pay to liturgical extensions of Eucharist, non-eucharistic devotions, and non-liturgical gatherings?

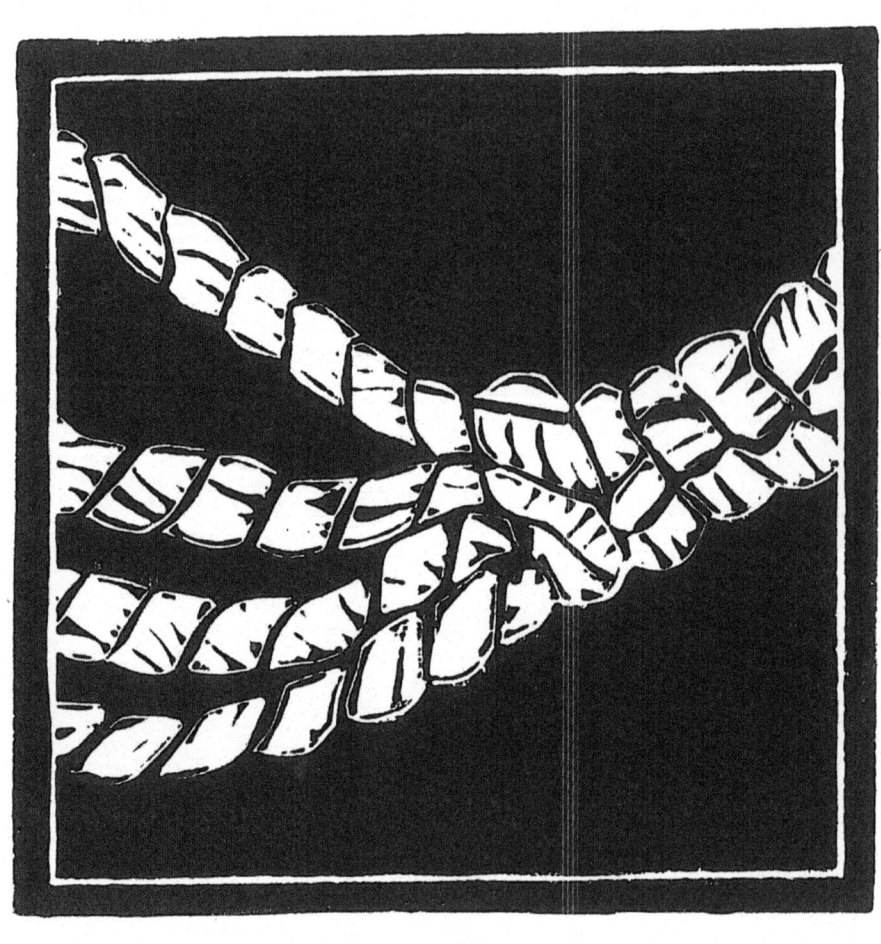

Chapter 11
Eucharist in the Local Church

Throughout this book the 'local' church is understood in a liturgical sense, that is, the community that assembles for Sunday Eucharist. In many cases this is simply the parish. For the sake of simplicity, this book assumes that a group of liturgical planners and ministers are responsible for the one or several Sunday Eucharists of the local community. Where this is not the case, we invite the reader to make the necessary adjustments to the points we make in this book.

Sometimes the term 'local' church is used to refer to a diocese since a diocese is geographically (locally) defined. But from a liturgical point of view, a diocese hardly ever, perhaps never, assembles for Sunday Eucharist and for that reason is better regarded as a regional grouping of local churches. Official church documents usually refer to a diocese headed by a bishop as a 'particular' church.[1]

This chapter is intended to bring together in a more explicit way the perspective on the church that runs through the previous chapters.

A real church with real symbols

The local community, the local church, that gathers for Eucharist is a real, not a notional church. The real church is not an idea of what the church should be as when we talk about the church as the Body of Christ, or the church as an institution, or the church that has endured through history. Nor is it a church which we believe *ought* to be there, as when we talk about how

---

1. For a description of the relationships between particular and universal church as understood in Vatican II's Dogmatic Constitution on the Church, see Joseph Joseph Femerée, 'Local Churches, Universal Church and Other Churches in *Lumen Gentium*', *Ecclesiology* 4/1 (2007): 52–67.

members of the church should love one another, or the commitment of the church to social justice, or the importance of good leadership in the church.

The church that gathers for Eucharist, the assembly of people who celebrate Eucharist, is a real church which is constituted by the communication of the participants with one another. If the communication is unchristian, then the church is to some degree distorted and evil. If the communication is flawed, then the church is flawed. If the communication is to some degree unintelligible, then the church is to some degree unintelligible. This church is a real church, not an ideal one.

Similarly the divine presence in Eucharist is a real one, not just an ideal or notional presence. The real presence of God is the liturgical communication that constitutes that Eucharist. This divine presence is so real that the ideas of what it ought to be or what we otherwise believe it should be do not overcome that reality or compensate for any shortcomings in that reality. If the communication is unchristian, then to that degree the divine presence is distorted. If the communication is quite seriously distorted, then we are in the presence of idols not of the God of Jesus Christ. The power of God distorted and idolatrous may be harmful rather than transformative for the human participants in Eucharist.

High level focus and ground level focus

Many of the books written about Eucharist, the official liturgical books like the Missal, and instructions from the Roman Congregation for Divine Worship, normally focus on Eucharist as a *type of liturgy* rather than on the Eucharist as a gathering of the local community. As a *type* of liturgy, Eucharist is distinct from other types of liturgy like Baptism or Reconciliation or Marriage or Funerals. It has its own particular meaning, it has a history, it has governing rules, it has scriptural foundations, it is backed by official church teaching—regardless of where it is celebrated or which community celebrates it. In this sense we can talk about, for example, bread and wine as the major symbols of Eucharist, the scriptural origins of Eucharist, the role of ministers in Eucharist, or the official rules governing the performance of Eucharist. This is a *high level* focus on Eucharist.

We adopt a rather different focus when we ask such questions as what music should we play next Sunday in St James's church at 10.00am, or whether we should change the way we do the Communion Rite so that people will appreciate it better, or what the key messages are in this coming Sunday's Readings, or how to overcome the problem of repetitious homilies in our community's Eucharists. Here we are talking not just about Eucharist as a type of liturgy but about *real instances* of Eucharist. Such questions may seem small matters in comparison with, for example, an in-depth study of the Eucharist in the New Testament or the publication of a new Roman Missal. They are perhaps relatively small questions, but they are not trivial. They are sacramental questions. Eucharist is a sacrament, a liturgical interaction of people who there encounter the divine presence effective in their lives. In this comparison, mere books fall away into relative unimportance.

The reality of Eucharist is not in books and documents *about* Eucharist but in the actual face-to-face interaction of real people in a real place at a real time. Through the symbols that make up that interaction people are nourished, provoked, changed and re-created in an encounter with the divine presence in Eucharist. These real symbols—the words, the actions, the movements, the gestures, the music, the use of bread and wine—are the ones that occupy the attention of liturgical ministers and planners. Liturgical ministers and planners in the local community need to know about Eucharist as a liturgical type, but their responsibility with this knowledge is to make the Eucharist liturgy work effectively as divine communication for a specific community of real people. We may call this a *ground level* focus on Eucharist.

Where high level focus and ground level focus intersect

Ideally these two ways of focusing on Eucharist should work together. When we focus on Eucharist as a type of liturgy we are concerned with the higher level of its meaning in the tradition of the church, what it ought to be like, and what its effects ought to be. When we focus on Eucharist as a face-to-face interaction of a gathering of believers we are concerned with the more grounded level of what a particular Eucharist means to these particular people, what it is actually like for them, and what effects it actually has on them. These two foci inform each other.

Liturgical planners in the local church will find however, and the more adventurous the planners are the more often it will occur, that there is sometimes a clash between the high level and the ground level focus. The classic circumstance of this clash is when a group of planners of a particular Eucharist are enthusiastic for a particular liturgical action until it is pointed out to them that this action is contrary to some official instruction on the liturgy: You may not change the words of the Collect Prayer! Only an ordained priest may give the homily! The priest has to receive Communion first! Should their hope for a better liturgical interaction go ahead anyway even if it breaks some of the official liturgical rules? Or have these liturgical planners misunderstood the real nature of Eucharist, inserted unchristian messages in their planned liturgy, rendered their Eucharist illicit or invalid, or simply made decisions they have no right to make?

When such clashes occur, the underlying issue is often regarded as one of ignorance. One side of the argument is that if the planners of Sunday Eucharists understood better the nature of Eucharist and had studied the liturgical books they would be better liturgists and not make such mistakes. The other side of the argument maintains that if the people who write the books and instructions on Eucharist better understood the lives of people and the ways they communicate they would write better books and instructions. The solution then is more and better education at both ends of the spectrum.

Better education is undoubtedly helpful, but liturgies are themselves acts of communication and therefore themselves educative. While education can take place in many formats, it seems odd to seek a solution to liturgical failure by looking to other forms of education such as classroom, study group, books, and electronic media while by-passing the educational nature of liturgy itself. For a more basic solution we will need to look further into the nature of liturgy itself.

The four strands of belonging

Our suggestion is that we can more constructively regard the issue here as one of 'belonging'. To whom does the liturgy belong? The Eucharist is an expression, an action, a feature perhaps, of the universal church (or at least of one of the major Rites of the universal church). In that sense it 'belongs' to the universal church as an important and integral part of the church's existence. Just as important though, and of special importance for liturgical planners and ministers, is that the Eucharist also 'belongs' to the local community that celebrates it. It belongs to the community of people who are actually, physically there engaged in that celebration of Eucharist at a particular time and in a particular place and will continue to do so regularly into the future.

Thus the Eucharist is a liturgical interaction with multiple belongings. It belongs to the universal church as well as to the local church but in somewhat different ways. Liturgical planners and ministers sit at the intersection of four strands of belonging and weave these four strands into the single complex cord of their continuing Sunday Eucharists.

One of these strands is the non-eucharistic *activities and organisation of the local church* that need to be brought into symbolic expression in the local

Sunday Eucharist so that it indeed becomes a 'summit' and 'source' of that community's life.

A second strand is the liturgical guardianship of the *central church authority* that interprets the multiple traditions of the universal church, oversees the unity of the universal church, and generates the liturgical books that govern standard liturgical performance.

A third strand derives from the varied and innovative liturgical practices of *other local churches* that are carried from one local church to another by travellers or through modern communications media and become a source of new ideas or warnings of failure.

A fourth strand is the *theological reflection* on liturgy that has no official or legal oversight but proposes the insights that result from historical and contemporary research.

The first strand: activities and organization of the local church

The people who make up a liturgical assembly are real people who have names and personalities and a history of living together, of cooperation and conflict. These are the people for whom planners and ministers have a particular responsibility and together have developed their own styles of communication. The Eucharist is one of the many kinds of gathering of a local Christian community. Normally the Sunday Eucharists are the most important of such gatherings in the sense that they both express and create the community in ways more powerful than other community actions. This is the primary sense in which we can say the liturgy is the 'summit' and 'source' of Christian life. What happens in that Sunday Eucharist gives us a good sense of what that community is like and what its basic beliefs are about itself, about its mission in the world, about the church at large, and about its God.

The Sunday Eucharist does not exist in a vacuum however. It expresses and creates the community, but it does so in interaction with other community liturgies and other community gatherings. Some of the people we meet at a community social gathering later in the week will be the same as those we met at Eucharist on Sunday. Many of the values expressed there will be the same. The leadership may overlap. Some of the topics of conversation may be the same and what is discussed there may have an impact on later Eucharists. Weekday Eucharists and other liturgical celebrations such as Baptisms and other sacraments as well as the many non-sacramental liturgies also express and create the community in a range of different ways that add to its richness.

As well as its liturgical gatherings, the community's leadership, its committees, its outreach organisation, its structures of education and formation, its ethnic communities, its special structures corresponding to gender or age differences, its celebratory social functions, its fundraising activities and so on are all contributors to the life of the community. We could expect that much of this organisational structure will appear in some way and from time to time in its Sunday Eucharists—in a variety of ways and with varying frequency, but nevertheless there.

We could expect, for example, that the community's leadership, its cultural diversity, its age groups and its educational programs would be somehow represented in its Eucharists. We discussed this earlier in the chapters on liturgical ministry and issues of representation. Some organizational features of the community might appear, for example, in Sunday Eucharists as notices or in the Prayer of the Faithful. Important here too is this local community's engagement with the wider world and the concerns there that are also its own. The comment of a visitor in a local Eucharist who found there no allusion at all to recent tragedies that had deeply affected neighbours and friends of that community provides an example of how a Sunday Eucharist can fail to represent the local community.

It is possible that the Sunday Eucharist may become largely divorced from all these other expressions of the community. This is the point at which the intimate relationship between the local community and its Eucharists becomes problematic and the Eucharist ceases to 'belong' to the local community in any recognisable way. This can occur in a variety of small symbolic ways that we have noted in earlier chapters, such as where the pastoral leader of the community is not the liturgical leader and seldom appears in the Sunday Eucharist in any leadership role. Similar problems are the invisible pastoral council, the community's teachers and other group leaders who merely attend Eucharist but are never acknowledged there in those roles.

This reaches an extreme form when the Sunday Eucharist is performed strictly according to the liturgical rubrics without any sense of its relationship to the local community, or when it is a largely solo performance by a priest who has little or no relationship to that local community apart from the Sunday Eucharist. Such cases can occur when a Sunday Eucharist scarcely belongs to the local community at all. A separation has occurred here between liturgy and life.

One of the important functions of local liturgical planners and ministers is to weave these wider local community interests into the symbolism of its Eucharists. Where this is successful the Eucharist is integral with the wider life of the community. It clearly and creatively 'belongs' to that local community.

The second strand: central church authority

The local church is itself part of a universal church that is expressed in a variety of ways—organisational structures, councils, representatives, and documents. But there is no such thing as a universal Eucharist. Liturgically speaking, the church achieves expression and becomes a real, visible, audible entity when some of its members gather liturgically especially in Eucharist.

Local liturgical planning is not intended to create a ghetto church or a provincial mentality that has no respect or responsibility for the wider church. It is not usually the intention of liturgical planners and ministers to finish up with a little, autonomous group of local people who go about doing their own thing in their own corner of the world with little reference to everyone else. Liturgical symbols declare our belonging to the universal church, our shared beliefs and mission, and our responsibility to the wider church and its representatives.

One of the major ways this universal link is maintained in the Catholic Church is through a central church authority, or better, several central church authorities, that have developed over the centuries and today are the several 'Rites' of the Catholic church. In our case, since we are considering the Roman Rite here, this central liturgical authority is represented by the Roman Congregation for Divine Worship. Some official liturgical decisions are also made at the regional level of dioceses and bishops' conferences.

Local churches need to take seriously the possibility that their liturgical practices may go astray. They may fail to be authentically Christian. They may become fixed in old patterns that no longer communicate to newer generations. They may lose their connections with the wider church and become focused only on themselves. The central and diocesan church authorities provide resources and oversight that are beyond the capacity of the local church.

Official liturgical books that provide resources, texts, and rules for liturgical performance become particularly important in time of reform. Once an official reform has been declared there remains the long process of reception by which official decisions are interpreted, implemented, ignored and sometimes resisted by the wider church. The church of the Roman Rite with its many local churches is now involved in this process of reception of the reforms of Vatican II.² Part of this process is maintaining a balance between the need for some centralisation of church decision-making and the inculturation of liturgy in local communities.³

An element of this process of reception that will most concern liturgical planners in the local church is that the central church authority's desire to reform can be overtaken by the desire for uniformity. The more prescriptive the official liturgical books become the more they run the risk that their prescribed symbols become insensitive or even offensive to the cultures of the local churches. Liturgical symbols have been developed over the centuries in Mediterranean and European cultures that are no longer the common ground of most of the local churches throughout the world. Local churches who do not share the cultural presuppositions of the central church authority may not agree that their own cultural symbols should be abandoned for those favoured by a central church authority.

Official church documents sometimes seem to imply that the only response required of local churches is obedience, except where explicit permission is given for local variations. But the function of local liturgical planners and ministers in their role as liturgists of the local church is more proactive and broader than simple submission. Their attitude is properly one of respect rather than of obedience. Respect implies taking seriously church authority with the knowledge and sensitivities that come from consultation with the wider church, but it does not mean reducing the local church to silent submission.

The official books and instructions of the central church authority make up a second important strand that liturgical planners and ministers weave into the symbolism of the local community.⁴

---

2. An article which seeks to discern successful and the unsuccessful reception in the liturgical reforms or Vatican II is Gerard Austin, 'The Reception of the Liturgical Reform of the Second Vatican Council', in *Liturgical Ministry* 17, Spring (2008): 49–57. For a discussion on the *General Instruction on the Roman Missal* measured by the principle of subsidiarity, see John M Huels, 'The New General Instruction of the Roman Missal: Subsidiarity or Uniformity?', in *Worship* 75/6 (2001): 482–511.
3. An overview of the definition and history of the term 'inculturation' as applied to liturgy is summarised in Anscar J Chupungco, 'Inculturation', in *The New SCM Dictionary of Liturgy and Worship*, edited by Paul Bradshaw (London: SCM Press, 2002), 244–51. Readers looking for further discussion of 'inculturation' of Eucharist may usefully consult Phillip Tovey, *Inculturation of Christian Worship: Exploring the Eucharist* (Aldershot, UK: Ashgate, 2004).
4. Readers wanting more information on liturgical law and how to implement it in diocesan administration, pastoral practice, and in the actual celebration of the liturgy may usefully

The third strand: the liturgical practices of other local churches

The link to the central church authority is not the only way the local church relates to the church universal. The universal church is made up of many local churches each with its Sunday gatherings. Liturgical symbols travel. They expand beyond the boundaries of the local church liturgies and are transported across into the liturgies of other communities. Travellers carry reports of their liturgical experiences from one place to another. As far as we know this is how Eucharist liturgies developed in the first place when there were no liturgical books and presumably few liturgy committee meetings. As people travelled they took their experience of Eucharist liturgies from one community to another and over time developed a typical form that has been passed down to us. Later, liturgical books were developed which further transported liturgical practices through the Christian world and sometimes eliminated previous practices.

Nowadays, electronic forms of communication mean that accounts of local church practices around the globe as well as decisions of councils and liturgical conferences spread new kinds of liturgical symbols or reinforce old ones. In many countries, liturgical symbols also travel between Christian denominations. People attend the liturgies of other Christian churches; if not their Sunday Eucharists, then their funerals and weddings. They also know about the liturgical practices of other churches through their friends and relatives who are members of those other churches.

We now have more access, in other words, to cultural and liturgical diversity throughout the world. This diversity provides resources for liturgical planners. Liturgical symbols from other places often need to be altered and integrated into the liturgical patterns of their new liturgical home. The movement of liturgical symbols becomes particularly rich but also problematic for liturgical planners when large numbers of people from other cultures join an existing local community. These new arrivals bring with them their own understandings and expectations of liturgical symbolism into their new community.

The third strand then that liturgical planners weave into the symbolism of their local Eucharists is this variety of liturgical practices that impact on the local church through accounts of the liturgies of other places or through the arrival of culturally diverse new members into the local community.

---

consult John M Huels, *Liturgy and Law: Liturgical Law in the System of Roman Catholic Canon Laws* (Montreal: Welson & Lafleur, 2006). The presentation of most interest to the general reader is probably the first chapter (9–62) entitled 'The Regulation of the Liturgy'.

The fourth strand: theological reflection

The fourth strand that liturgical planners weave into the symbolism of the local Eucharists is the theological reflection that is carried out by people who give time and energy to liturgical study and research. These are self-critical and reflective studies which are not the same as official church teaching, nor are they the same as the communication that occurs within the liturgies themselves. There are many books and internet sites that are concerned with this. Liturgical planners need to be familiar with some of these that will serve to critique and enhance their own liturgies.

This book is itself an example of such theological reflection. It is a critical reflection on our current liturgical practices in the light of contemporary research and experiment. It is intended to inform liturgical planning and ministry, to reinforce some existing liturgical practices and to critique others. Such reflections constitute the fourth strand that liturgical planners weave into the symbolism of their Sunday Eucharists.

Conclusion

The Sunday Eucharist contributes to the development of a real, local church that is constituted by the way people communicate with one another and enlivened by a real presence of the Divine. We have suggested that this goal can be reached realistically if liturgical planners and ministers weave together four strands that together make up the symbolism of the Sunday Eucharist. These are the normal activities and organization of their own local church, the documents of the central and diocesan church authority, the liturgical practices of other local churches, and the literature that brings us the results of theological research and reflection.

Key questions:

1) What is meant by the 'local' church, and what other kinds of church are there?
2) Liturgical planners may be seen as weaving four strands of belonging in the church. What are these four strands?
3) What are the current major issues in our local church community?

Index

A

Abuse, 19, 107, 109.
Access/accessible, 5, 7, 8, 13, 17, 45, 46, 63, 65, 80, 91, 115, 131.
Action, 2, 3, 5, 6, 7, 8, 9, 11, 13, 15, 16, 17, 18, 20, 24, 25, 26, 28, 29, 31, 36, 39, 42, 48, 53, 54, 56, 59, 60, 61, 66, 70, 74, 77, 78, 81, 82, 89, 90, 108, 113, 114, 115, 116, 118, 119, 125, 126, 127.
Addressing God, 40, 54, 77.
Advent, 100, 103, 109, 125.
Age, 4, 6, 7, 15, 16, 28, 37, 38, 40, 52, 54, 56, 70, 76, 77, 86, 87, 93, 96, 128,
Announcement/s, 9, 40, 41, 42, 78, 79.
Architecture, 36 81.
Assembly, 9, 23, 24, 25, 29, 41, 32, 35, 36, 37, 38, 39, 40, 42, 43, 45, 46, 48, 49, 50, 52, 53, 54, 55, 55, 56, 60, 61, 62, 63, 64, 66, 67, 69, 70, 73, 75, 76, 77, 78, 79, 80, 81, 82, 83, 85, 86, 87, 88, 89, 90, 91, 92, 93, 94, 95, 97, 107, 112, 113-14, 116, 124, 127.
Atmosphere, 5, 25, 36, 63, 78, 85, 97.
Attentive, 3, 48, 61, 64, 101.
Attention, 2, 3, 6, 8, 11, 13, 14, 15, 16, 17, 18, 20, 23, 24, 25, 26, 31, 39, 40, 45, 47, 53, 55, 63, 69, 76, 77, 78, 80, 89, 94, 95, 96, 100, 101, 102, 104, 105, 106, 107, 108, 111, 116, 117, 119, 120, 125.
Attitude/s, 13, 14, 19, 25, 47, 55, 61, 64, 78, 79, 82, 83, 86, 95, 113, 130.
Attractive, 17, 63.
Audience, 88.
Authority, 14, 15, 19, 51, 68, 129, 130, 131, 132.

B

Bearer of gifts, 26, 59, 69.
Beautiful, 1, 17, 63, 87, 94.

Beauty, 1, 93, 94.
Beliefs, 17, 18, 19, 28, 99, 105, 106, 118, 119, 127, 129.
Belong, 4, 7, 23, 25, 28, 37, 85, 126, 128, 129.
Belonging, 1, 5, 20, 36, 66, 67, 68, 70, 71, 86, 126, 129, 132.
Benediction, 112, 113.
Bible, the, 17, 27, 45, 46, 47 48, 108.
Bishop, 45, 76, 123, 129.
Blessing, 9, 40, 41, 42, 78, 79, 107, 108.
Body of Christ, 14, 29, 43, 50, 123.
Bowing, 64.
Bread, 17, 46, 51, 59, 60, 61, 65, 66, 67, 75, 81, 82, 108, 113, 114, 115, 124, 125.

C

Calendar, 51, 89, 99, 100, 101, 102, 103-109, 104, 105, 106, 107, 108, 109.
Cantor, 26, 54, 86, 88, 94.
Catholic, 4, 12, 13, 61, 85, 90, 115, 129, 131.
Celebrant, 23, 36.
Celebrate, 2, 4, 13, 14, 20, 23, 24, 31, 99, 102, 106, 112, 113, 117, 124, 126.
Celebration, 14, 20, 29, 35, 37, 39, 40, 41, 59, 65, 85, 87, 96, 99, 100, 101, 103, 105, 106, 108, 109, 112, 113, 117-18, 126, 127, 130.
Challenge, 4, 16, 37, 48, 49, 73, 101, 104, 109, 118.
Change, 4, 5, 11, 12, 13, 16, 28, 30, 31, 38, 41, 42, 43, 49, 50, 56, 68, 75, 77, 81, 82, 85, 99, 101, 104, 107, 115, 116, 124, 125.
Choir, 1, 28, 85, , 86, 88, 91, 94, 95.
Choir leader, 1, 26, 85, 86, 87, 88, 91, 94, 95.

Christ, 7, 8, 14, 23, 24, 29, 43, 50, 61, 64, 74, 75, 76, 77, 100-101, 109, 115, 123, 124.

Christian, 3, 4, 5, 8, 11, 12, 14, 15, 19, 20, 23, 25, 27, 28, 31, 32, 40, 41, 43, 50, 51, 52, 55, 61, 65, 67, 68, 71, 76, 77, 87, 90, 92, 93, 96, 99, 100, 101, 102, 104, 105, 106, 109, 112-114, 118, 127, 129, 130, 131.

Christmas, 100, 101, 102, 103, 109.

Church, the, 3, 7, 11, 12, 13, 14, 15, 16, 17, 18, 19, 20, 23, 25, 27, 36, 37, 39, 50, 61, 62, 63, 64, 65, 68, 76, 81, 87, 92, 93, 101, 102, 105, 107, 108, 109, 111, 112, 115, 117, 118, 123, 124, 125, 126, 127, 129, 130, 131, 132.

Collect Prayer,35, 36, 38, 40, 78, 89, 108, 125.

Collector, 26, 29.

Colour, use of, 17, 64, 67, 102, 103.

Commissioning, 29, 30, 31, 39, 96.

Communal, 2, 4, 6, 26, 52, 53, 56, 63, 80, 94, 96, 99, 107, 114, 115, 117.

Communicate, 12, 17, 18, 29, 36, 49, 52, 55, 56, 74, 79, 80, 119, 126, 129, 132.

Communication, 15, 16, 17, 18, 19, 20, 29, 30, 52, 56, 74, 80, 115, 124, 125, 126, 127, 131, 132.

Communion, 8, 29, 35, 41, 59, 65, 66, 67, 68, 69, 70, 71, 78, 79, 80, 81, 82, 89, 111, 112, 113, 114, 115, 116, 117, 120, 124, 125.

Communion minister, 28, 29, 65, 66, 67, 68, 69, 70, 71, 81, 82, 114,

Communion of the Sick, 111, 112, 113, 117.

Community, 3, 4, 5, 6, 7, 8, 9, 11, 14, 15, 18, 19, 20, 23, 24, 27, 28, 29, 30, 31, 32, 36, 37, 38, 39, 40, 41, 42, 43, 49, 50, 51, 52, 53, 56, 60, 61, 62, 63, 65, 66, 67, 68, 70, 71, 74, 75, 76, 79, 81, 82, 86, 87, 89, 90, 91, 93-100, 104, 105, 106, 107, 109, 111-15, 117, 118, 119, 120, 123-132.

Competent, 27, 52, 76.

Competence, 27, 28, 30, 31, 55, 69, 70, 76, 77, 80, 96.

Concelebration, 65.

Congregation, 1, 2, 6, 23, 37, 38, 46, 47, 48, 50, 53, 54, 56, 59, 60, 61m 62m 63, 64, 65, 66, 73, 74, 77, 81, 82, 86, 89, 91, 94, 95, 106, 114, 116, 117, 124, 129.

Contemporary, 5, 12, 13, 14, 15, 20, 24, 26, 37, 38, 46, 47, 52, 54, 60, 67, 68, 70, 71, 73, 74, 76, 81, 87, 92, 94, 101, 115, 127.

Context, 11, 14, 15, 20, 31, 48.

Cooperate, 118.

Cooperative, 81, 112, 118.

Crossroads, 11, 12, 20.

Culture, 2, 3, 6, 7, 13, 14, 15, 16, 36, 38, 40, 60, 64, 67, 69, 70, 76, 77, 85, 87, 92, 93, 94, 95, 96, 101, 105, 117, 130, 131.

Cultural, 3, 4, 6, 12, 14, 15, 19, 20, 36, 37, 60, 64, 67, 69, 77, 85, 86, 87, 92, 95, 96, 100, 101, 105, 106, 108, 109, 114, 116, 118, 130, 131.

D

Decision, 4, 6, 14, 24, 29, 30, 37, 40, 41, 45, 60, 64, 65, 68, 85, 92, 93, 105, 106, 107, 118, 119, 126, 129, 130, 131.

Dialogue, 62, 63, 64, 81, 95.

Dimensions of Eucharist, 8, 16, 18, 19, 20, 29, 50, 51, 52, 70, 104, 111.

Diocese, 5, 20, 37, 123, 129.

Discern/discernment, 6, 27, 104, 105, 106, 109, 130.

Disciple, 7, 50, 61, 103.

Discriminatory, 6, 46.

Dismissal, 31, 40, 42, 78, 79.

Distribute, 60, 65, 66.

Distribution, 51, 65, 114.

Divine, 7, 24, 38, 45, 56, 65, 66, 67, 68, 70, 87, 104, 117, 124, 125, 129, 132.

Divine presence, 45, 66, 67, 124, 125, 132.

Dress, 4, 17, 64, 111,

E

Easter, 100, 101, 102, 103, 109.

Ecological issues, 8, 51, 104.

Economic, socio, 4, 6, 7, 51, 52, 76.

Education, 30, 52, 55, 74, 126, 128.

Educational, 27, 29, 80, 126, 128.

Effect, 18, 27, 29, 30, 59, 63, 68, 74, 79, 93, 106, 115, 125

Effectiveness, 125.

Efficacious, effective, 17, 18, 27, 35, 108 118, 125,

Elderly, 4, 6, 15, 92.

Empower, 3, 9.

Engage, 1, 2, 5, 8, 9, 15, 16, 25, 26, 37, 39, 49, 52, 53, 63, 76, 77, 78, 86, 88, 90, 106, 126,

Engagement, 9, 25, 37, 38, 54, 56, 89, 93, 109, 128.

English, 38, 45, 46, 63, 64, 94.

Entrance, 27, 35, 36, 37, 47, 78, 89.

Environment, environmental, 4, 104, 118.

Ethnic, 4, 5, 27, 28, 40, 52, 128.
Ethnicity, 6, 54, 56, 74.
Eucharistic Prayer, 59, 60, 61, 62, 63, 64, 70, 81, 88, 89, 90, 95, 113, 114, 115.
Evaluation, 117.
Expectation/s, 16, 24, 36, 48, 74, 76, 96, 107, 131.

F

Facing, 31, 64, 74.
Fail, 1, 2, 7, 18, 43, 51, 62, 96,
Failure, 1, 16, 43, 60, 127.
Father, God, the, 38, 77, 81.
Father's Day, 106
Feedback, 48, 63.
Formal, 35, 36, 37, 38, 39, 41, 42, 63, 77, 78, 79, 119.
Formation, 19, 20, 23, 29, 30, 32, 50, 55, 69, 79, 96, 128,
Funeral, 25, 124m 131.

G

Gather, 43, 65, 70, 76, 112, 123, 124, 129.
Gathering, 9, 23, 27, 35, 36, 37, 38, 39, 40, 41, 42, 43, 45, 47, 48, 59, 75, 78, 79, 89, 95, 108, 111, 112, 113, 114, 115, 116, 118, 119, 124, 125, 127, 128, 131.
Gender, 4, 7, 28, 38, 45, 54, 56, 70, 74, 77, 128.
Generation, 12, 14, 15, 85, 99, 118.
Gestures, 25, 64, 77, 89, 125.
Gifts, 7, 26, 29, 35, 59, 60, 69, 71, 80, 81, 95, 114.
Globalizing, 107.
Gloria, 36, 38, 89, 94, 95.
Goal, 8, 27, 61, 76, 86, 87, 132.
God, 2, 3, 5, 7, 8, 9, 17, 18, 19, 38, 39, 40, 41, 42, 43, 50, 51, 54, 56, 61, 62, 65, 70, 74, 78, 81, 82, 87, 93, 94, 95, 97, 100, 103, 104, 112, 124, 127.
Gospel, the, 45, 47, 49, 53, 80, 92, 102, 112.
Grace, 7, 17, 60, 65, 70.
Gracious, 25, 28.
Greeting, 36, 37, 38, 78, 89.
Greeter, 37.
Ground-level focus, 124, 125.
Guardian, 4, 5, 42, 127.

H

Harmful, 18, 29, 124.
Hearing, 17, 87.
Hierarchical, 19, 65, 76.
High-level focus, 124,
Historical, 11, 12, 13, 14, 15, 20, 31, 47, 64, 92, 100, 102, 104, 105, 111, 127.
Homily, 41, 45, 47, 48, 49, 50, 51, 52, 53, 54, 55, 56, 80, 90, 93, 108, 125.
Homilist, 48, 49, 50, 51, 52, 53, 55, 80.
Hospitality, 3, 4, 5, 36, 37, 87, 119.
Hospitable, 1, 3, 5, 9, 11, 31, 36, 40, 54, 56, 70, 73, 78, 87, 92, 96.
Host, 4, 5, 9, 40, 42, 61, 67, 79, 112, 134.
Hymn, 35, 36, 37, 38, 86, 89, 90-95.

I

Identity, 4, 5, 15, 19, 20, 32, 36, 37, 39, 40, 42, 43, 52, 66, 67, 70, 79, 87, 89, 94, 95, 97, 99, 106, 109, 119.
Identity formation, 16, 19, 20, 32, 42, 52, 79, 87.
Image, 38, 39, 42, 47, 54, 61, 77, 78, 81, 93, 101-104.
Impact, 3, 17, 25, 47, 53, 65, 67, 73, 81, 83, 85, 93, 97, 113, 114, 116, 117, 119, 120, 127, 131.
Inclusive, 1, 3, 5, 6, 7, 9, 11, 15, 31, 36, 37, 38, 45, 46, 54, 56, 62, 70, 73, 77, 78, 81, 87, 92-96.
Inculturation, 13, 14, 60, 76, 92, 130.
Informal, 36, 37, 77, 78.
Informality, 37.
Interaction, 20, 28, 31, 36, 48, 74, 125, 126, 127.
Interior, 2, 53, 86.
Interpreter, 51.
Interpretation, 9, 12, 28, 48, 49, 50, 52, 55, 56, 64, 67, 80, 101-104.
Invite, 9, 64, 79, 89, 96, 102, 103, 123.
Invitation, 16, 41, 54, 116.

J

Jesus, 20, 23, 61, 93, 100, 101, 103, 108, 112, 124.
Justice, 5, 8, 42, 105, 118, 119, 124.

K

Key features, 1, 3, 9, 56, 120.
Kinaesthesia, 17.
Kneeling, 64, 116.
Kyrie, 36, 94, 95.

L

Language, 4, 5, 18, 38, 45, 46, 47, 54, 55, 62, 63, 64, 70, 77, 78, 81, 94, 111, 112.
Leader, 1, 2, 5, 14, 20, 23, 24, 25, 26, 27, 28, 30, 31, 36, 40, 42, 55, 64, 70, 77–88, 90, 91, 93, 94, 95, 96, 106–108, 116, 128.
Leadership, 69, 73, 74, 75, 76, 79, 81, 82, 83, 114, 116, 124, 127, 128.
Lectern, 46, 47.
Lectionary, the, 45, 46, 47, 52, 53, 55, 56.
Legitimate, 16, 30, 71, 107.
Lent, 100, 102, 103, 109
Lifestyle, 6, 19, 28, 52, 55, 70, 76, 96.
Listen, listening/listeners, 2, 27, 46, 47, 48, 49, 52, 53, 86, 89, 95.
Litany, 36, 78, 88, 89, 95.
Liturgical books, 12, 20, 79, 95, 108, 114, 124, 125, 126, 127, 129, 132.
Liturgical planners, the, 3, 5, 6, 8, 12, 13, 14, 15, 16, 17, 18, 19, 20, 23, 24, 25, 26, 30, 31, 37, 38, 40–48, 51, 52, 54, 55, 59, 60, 61, 62, 63, 64, 65, 66, 67, 68, 69, 74, 76, 77, 79, 80, 82, 85, 86, 87, 88, 90, 91, 92, 94, 95, 96, 97, 100, 101, 104, 105, 106, 107, 108–120, 123, 125, 127–130, 131, 132.
Liturgy, the, 1, 2, 3, 5, 6, 7, 8, 9, 12, 13, 14, 15, 16, 19, 20, 23, 24, 25, 26, 28, 29, 30, 31, 35, 36, 37, 38, 39, 40, 42, 43, 45, 46, 47, 48, 49, 50, 51, 52, 53, 54, 55, 56, 59, 60, 61, 62, 66, 69, 70–96, 102, 103, 104, 107, 108, 112–119, 124–128, 130, 131.
Liturgy of the Word, the, 35, 39, 45f, 59, 61, 62, 75, 79, 80f, 111–116.
Local, 41, 43, 45, 50, 61, 62, 63, 75, 76, 82, 87, 90, 95, 99, 100, 102, 105, 107, 109, 111–118, 123f.
location, locality, 4, 5, 105, 109, 112.
Look, 14, 26, 27, 35, 51, 53, 63, 65, 69, 73, 79, 80, 82, 103, 113, 114, 120, 126, 130.
Lord, 38, 46, 87, 89.

M

Mass, the, 2, 8, 24, 35, 39, 53, 61, 73, 74, 94.
Meaning, 2, 3, 6, 16, 17, 18, 27, 47, 52, 55, 70, 89, 93, 100, 105, 112, 117, 124, 125.
Meditative, 86, 95, 116.
Member, 4, 5, 6, 7, 9, 11, 18, 23, 25, 36, 40, 41, 49, 51, 53, 54, 59, 64, 65, 66, 67, 68, 69, 78, 80, 87, 88, 90, 91, 99, 105, 106, 118, 124, 129, 131.
membership, 4.
Message, 36, 42, 49, 50, 51, 52, 62, 69, 74, 77, 93, 105, 106, 108, 112, 118, 124, 126.
Ministers, 3, 4, 5, 7, 8, 9, 14, 15, 17, 18, 19, 20, 23, 24, 25, 26, 27, 28, 29, 30, 31, 32, 37, 38, 39, 40, 42, 47, 52–55, 65, 66, 67, 68, 69, 70, 71, 73, 74, 75, 78, 79, 80, 81, 82, 88, 89, 91, 92, 96, 107, 114–118, 123–130, 132.
Ministry, 2, 5, 7, 8, 9, 11, 12, 18, 23, 25, 26, 27, 28, 29, 30, 31, 32, 41, 42, 52, 53, 55, 61, 69–78, 80, 81, 82, 87, 90, 96, 103, 114, 116, 117, 118, 128, 130.
Mission, 5, 8, 9, 20, 26, 35, 40, 41, 42, 43, 50, 54, 75, 79, 93, 105, 108, 109, 127, 129.
Missionary, 8, 9, 31, 41, 42, 50, 79, 81.
Mother's Day, 106.
Movement, 4, 12, 17, 25, 64, 65, 66, 80, 89, 99, 102, 107, 108, 109, 111, 117, 125, 131.
Music, 6, 17, 35, 40, 54, 55, 73, 85f, 124, 125.
Musician, 26, 28, 40, 78, 86, 87, 88, 91, 94, 96, 97,

N

Negotiation, 16, 18, 19, 20, 70, 97, 115.
Newcomer, 4, 5.
Noise, 17, 53, 86.
Non-eucharistic, 11, 117, 118, 119, 120, 126.
Non-liturgical gatherings, 111, 118, 119, 120.

O

Object symbol, 17, 46, 61, 67, 88, 89, 101, 107, 108, 112.
Observers, 24, 25.
Observing, 2.
Odour, 17.
Official, 12, 13, 19, 24, 38, 40, 41, 46, 63, 67, 77, 79, 81, 85, 95, 114, 115, 124, 125, 126, 127, 129, 130, 132.
Options, 24, 46, 56.

Order, 14, 16, 19, 42, 54, 67, 68, 97, 107.
Orientation, 9, 37, 38, 39, 40, 43, 99.
Outgoing, 1, 3, 7, 8, 9, 11, 15, 31, 50, 54, 56, 70, 73, 75, 87.
Outreach, 8, 9, 40, 41, 42, 43, 56, 79, 81, 82, 87, 96, 128.

P

Parish, 4, 9, 123.
Participant, 1, 2, 3, 5, 7, 8, 9, 14, 17, 18, 19, 24, 25, 43, 39, 52, 53, 66, 73, 74, 79, 89, 116, 117, 124.
Participate, 6, 9, 24, 42, 66, 82.
Participation, 1f, 11, 15,
passive, passivity20, 24, 25, 26, 31, 32, 35, 36, 37, 39, 42, 46, 52, 54, 60, 61, 62, 63, 64, 65, 66, 70, 74, 78, 81, 82, 83, 85, 86, 87, 88, 89, 91, 92, 94, 114, 115, 116.
Penitence, 36, 40, 64, 78.
Penitential, 39, 78, 88, 89, 95.
Pentecost, 100, 102, 103.
Performance, 2, 6, 17, 18, 27, 29, 30, 63, 64, 74, 87, 88, 116, 124, 128, 129.
Permission, 105, 107, 108, 109.
Perspective, 86.
Phases of Eucharist, 35, 59, 73, 75, 95, 97, 99, 113,
Pilgrim, 5.
Place, 2, 4, 5, 9, 13, 14, 15, 16, 18, 19, 23, 36, 39, 40, 55, 62, 65, 68, 74, 75, 77, 78, 79, 85, 90, 92, 95, 97, 99, 101, 103, 105, 109, 113, 117, 119, 125, 126, 131.
Planner, planning, 3, 5, 6, 8, 12–20, 23, 24, 25, 26, 30, 31, 37, 38, 40, 41, 42, 45, 46, 47, 48, 51, 52, 54, 55, 59, 60–74, 76, 77, 79, 80, 82, 85, 86, 87, 88, 90, 91, 92, 93, 94, 95, 97, 100, 101, 104, 105, 106, 107, 108, 111–120, 123, 125–130, 131, 132.
Political, 15, 25, 51, 52, 54, 76, 89, 92, 104, 106.
Posture, 4, 17, 25, 53, 54, 64, 89, 111.
Power/powerrful, 1, 3, 8, 9, 18, 19, 20, 30, 36, 38, 41, 51, 67, 68, 70, 102, 105, 107, 108, 109, 116, 119, 124, 127.
Praise, 38, 39, 61, 78, 89, 95.
Prayer, 2, 3, 9, 25, 26, 35, 38, 40, 53, 54, 62, 77, 78, 81, 88, 97, 106, 108, 112, 117, 125.
Prayer after Communion, 41, 79,
Prayer, Eucharistic, 59, 60, 61, 62, 63, 64, 70, 81, 88, 89, 90, 93, 95, 113, 114, 115.
Prayer of the Faithful, 39, 45, 53, 55, 56, 80, 116, 128.
Prayerful, 25, 36, 54, 79.
Preacher, 26.
Preparation, 29, 30, 32, 49, 50, 56, 59, 60, 69, 71, 72, 75, 100.
Preparation of gifts, 29, 59, 60, 69, 71.
Presentation, 8, 19, 27, 28, 29, 30, 31, 47, 49, 50, 55, 60, 69, 70, 71, 78, 80, 82, 92, 95, 128.
Presider, 26, 31, 40, 41, 73, 74, 75, 76, 77, 82, 114.
Presiding, 66.
Priest, 2, 3, 17, 23, 26, 27, 40, 51, 52, 56, 59, 60, 62, 63, 64, 66, 67, 68, 70, 73, 74, 76, 78, 80, 81, 82, 86, 90, 92, 107, 112, 117, 125, 128.
Process, 4,5, 27, 28, 30, 31, 32, 56, 63, 68, 71, 82, 90, 94, 96, 97, 103, 106, 107, 129, 130.
Procession, 46, 47, 53, 55, 59, 60, 78, 89, 108, 114, 117,
Proclaim, 77, 81, 103.
Proclamation, 17, 46.
Profession of Faith, 53, 54, 55.
Psalm, 53, 89, 115.

Q

Qualification, 23, 27, 28, 30, 32, 56, 69, 70, 71, 96, 97.
Qualified, 52, 97.

R

Racist, 18.
Reader, 3, 8, 12, 13, 15, 26, 27, 28, 37, 46, 47, 53, 55, 56, 80, 85, 86, 87, 90, 100, 102, 103, 123, 130, 131.
Reading, 6, 27, 28, 39, 41–56, 80, 89, 100, 103, 106, 112, 124.
Real, 36, 38, 48, 53, 74, 75, 118, 123, 124, 125, 126, 127, 129, 132.
Receive, 19, 41, 48, 52, 66–69, 89, 125.
Reception, 13, 65, 67, 68, 81, 129, 130.
Receptive, 18, 25.
Recipients, 24, 25, 26.
Recruitment, 30, 31, 32, 69, 75, 96.
Reform, 12, 13, 26, 87, 92, 113, 129, 130.
Reign of God, 7, 8, 42.
Renewal, 7, 12, 13, 20, 31, 87.
Repetition, 37, 38.
Repetitious, 38, 124.

Representation, 19, 27, 28, 29, 30, 31, 55, 69, 70, 74, 76, 80, 82, 96, 128.
Representative, 70, 129.
Research, 127, 132.
Responsibility, 7, 15, 18, 24, 26, 36, 40, 52, 64, 73, 93, 108, 125, 127, 129.
Restoration, 12, 13, 20, 31.
Retirement, 30, 31, 32, 55, 56, 69, 71, 96.
Rhythm, 39.
Rite, 2, 4, 9, 12, 13, 14, 36, 37, 38, 39, 45, 46, 47, 60, 63, 69, 73, 82, 85, 88, 94, 96, 105, 129.
Rite, Communion, 41, 60, 65f, 81, 82, 113, 114, 116, 124.
Rite of Gathering, Gathering Rite, 23, 35f, 38, 39, 40, 42, 45, 47, 48, 59, 75, 78, 89, 95, 112, 115.
Rite of Sending, Sending Rite, 23, 35f, 42, 59, 75, 78, 79, 112, 115, 116.
Ritual, 2, 7, 11, 12, 15, 16, 18, 20, 25, 31, 60, 66, 67, 69, 85, 86, 96, 99, 107, 111.
Role, 6, 16, 19, 23, 24, 25, 26, 30, 36, 40, 42, 60, 64, 66, 68, 69, 70, 73, 74, 75, 77, 78, 79, 80, 81, 82, 88, 90, 94, 96, 97, 109, 124, 128.
Rubrics, 67, 95, 115, 128.
Rules, 11, 16, 20, 74, 124, 126, 129.

S

Sacrament/s, 8, 17, 18, 19, 41, 51, 82, 105, 111, 112, 113, 117, 125, 127.
Sacred, 8, 65, 66, 68, 74, 85, 87, 92.
Saints, 108, 109.
Sanctuary, 65, 74, 81.
Scripture, 6, 9, 17, 20, 26, 27, 28, 39, 41, 45–56, 75, 80, 89, 95, 100, 103, 106, 115, 116.
Season/s, 39, 48, 51, 95, 99, 100, 101, 102, 103, 104, 105, 107, 108, 109.
Self-revelation, 17.
Sending, 9, 23, 35f, 59, 69, 75, 78, 79, 82, 95, 108, 112, 113, 115, 116.
Sending Prayer, 9, 41, 79,
Service, 3, 7, 8, 27, 28, 29, 30, 31, 51, 53, 55, 65, 67, 70, 71.
Sexist, 18, 45, 46, 62, 118.
Sight, 17, 103.
Sign, 25, 38, 81,
Signify, 18.
Silent, 2, 6, 54, 77, 86, 130.

Silence/d, 19, 36, 52, 53, 54, 55, 77, 80, 86, 87, 95, 116.
Singing, 1, 25, 28, 54, 63, 85, 86, 87, 88, 89, 90, 91, 94, 95.
Sitting, 25, 64, 77.
Skill, 1, 6, 7, 26, 27, 28, 29, 37, 40, 49, 55, 60, 63, 69, 74, 76, 77, 80, 96, 117.
Social, 4, 8, 9, 12, 19, 23, 30, 37, 45, 51, 68, 78, 104, 105, 109, 118, 119, 124, 127.
Society, 3, 9, 12, 28, 50, 51, 52, 56, 68, 76, 93, 104, 105, 106, 109.
Socio-economic, 4, 6, 7.
Solo singing, 1, 63, 86, 88, 91, 94, 95.
Source, 7, 8, 24, 52, 82, 86, 93, 104, 105, 119, 127.
Space, 17, 25, 36, 37, 47, 99, 100, 111.
Speech, 17, 77.
Spirit of God, 7, 23, 39, 43, 48, 50, 61, 77, 93, 97, 104, 109,
Spiritual, 27, 50, 114, 117,
Spirituality, 45, 51, 54, 66, 74, 100, 111, 118,
Standing, 25, 64, 77, 108, 116,
Strands of belonging, 126f, 132.
Structure, 24, 31, 36, 37, 39, 41, 51, 59, 63, 76, 89, 95, 128, 129.
Summit, 7, 8, 127.
Sunday, 2, 12, 14, 15, 16, 19, 24, 26, 29, 30, 39, 40, 43, 48, 49, 50, 51, 52, 56, 63, 66, 71, 74, 76, 78, 79, 85, 87, 88, 89, 90, 91, 92, 93, 94, 97, 99, 100, 102, 104, 105, 108, 109, 111–120, 123, 124, 126, 127, 128, 131, 132.
Symbol, 2, 5, 6, 7, 8, 9, 17, 19, 46, 53, 65, 66, 67, 68, 71, 101–109, 111, 114, 117, 123, 125, 129, 130, 131.
Symbolic, 3, 9, 15, 16, 17, 20, 30, 47, 59, 61, 64, 65, 66, 69, 70, 76, 82, 88, 89, 90, 91, 99, 104, 112, 113, 126, 128,

T

Task, 5, 14, 42, 43, 47, 52, 53, 75, 80, 104, 109.
Thanksgiving, 23, 39, 61, 62, 70, 81, 82, 112, 113.
Theology, 24, 30, 38, 60, 77, 93, 94.
Theological, 8, 61, 67, 68, 73, 76, 93, 94, 102, 106, 127, 132.
Touch, 17, 65, 78.
Tradition, 3, 11, 12, 17, 18, 20, 36, 37., 47, 54, 60, 67, 68, 77, 87, 92, 95, 100, 102, 103, 104, 108, 109, 115, 119, 125, 127.

Training, 30, 49, 55, 56, 68, 71, 75, 76, 82, 96, 114.
Transformation, 8, 16, 17, 20, 29, 50, 51, 52, 56, 87, 92,
Transformative, 18, 30, 32, 52, 74, 97, 124.
Translation, 38, 45, 46, 94.

U

Understanding, 1, 2, 4, 9, 15, 17, 23, 24, 29, 46, 47, 48, 50, 52, 70, 81, 85, 86, 93, 95, 102, 109.
Unison, 1, 24, 53.
Universal, 14, 20, 39, 62, 115, 123, 126, 127, 129, 131.
Usher, 26, 27, 37, 66, 78.

V

Values, 17, 18, 19, 28, 99, 105, 106, 109, 118, 119, 127,
Variety, 2, 4, 7, 26, 31, 36, 40, 52, 55, 56, 76, 77, 82, 87, 90, 92, 96, 99, 114, 115, 116, 117, 128, 129, 131.
Vatican II, Vatican Council, 3, 7, 12, 74, 113, 130.
Vision, 4, 100, 117.
Volunteer, 26, 27.

W

Weekday, 109, 111, 116, 119, 120, 127.
Weekly Eucharist, 49, 85, 99, 109, 112.
Welcome, 3, 4, 35, 37, 38, 40, 43, 76, 78, 79, 117, 119.
Wine, 17, 46, 51, 59, 60, 61, 65, 66, 67, 75, 81, 822, 108, 114, 124, 125.
Witness, 7, 25, 27, 28, 29, 30, 31, 55, 69, 70, 76, 80, 82, 96.
Word, Liturgy of, 23, 35, 39, 40, 45f, 59, 61, 62, 75, 79, 80, 81, 83, 95, 112, 115, 120.
Word and Communion, 111, 113, 114, 115, 116, 120.
World, 7, 8, 15, 20, 35, 37, 40, 41, 42, 43, 50, 54, 64, 79, 87, 95, 100, 102, 103, 104, 109, 112, 127, 128, 130, 131.
Worship, 2, 3, 5, 7, 8, 12, 13, 18, 38, 40, 51, 60, 85, 86, 87, 92, 102, 115, 117, 118, 124, 128, 130.

Lightning Source UK Ltd.
Milton Keynes UK
UKOW04f2157220917
309708UK00001B/153/P